HARRY'S WAR

About the author

Robert Jobson is an award-winning journalist and author. *Harry's War* is his third book about the British Royal Family. His first, *Diana: Closely Guarded Secret*, written with Princess Diana's former Scotland Yard bodyguard Ken Wharfe, is an acclaimed Number One *Sunday Times* bestseller as well as a top-ten *New York Times* bestseller. His second book, *William's Princess*, is the first definitive account of Prince William's relationship with Kate Middleton and analyses how he will reshape the British monarchy.

After graduating from the University of Kent at Canterbury in History and English, the author began his career in journalism. His became royal reporter with the *Sun* newspaper in 1991 and later joined the *Daily Express*, where he went on to become royal and diplomatic editor as well as assistant editor. In 2005 he was awarded the coveted Scoop of the Year for breaking the world exclusive in the London *Evening Standard* that the Prince of Wales and his long-term mistress Camilla Parker Bowles were to wed, the first time a journalist and not Buckingham Palace has announced a royal engagement. He is currently Royal Editor of the *News of the World*.

As CNN's royal commentator, he joined the anchors live on screen to deliver global coverage of the wedding of the Prince of Wales and the Duchess of Cornwall, the Queen's Golden Jubilee celebrations and the historic funeral of Her Majesty the late Queen Mother. He has also appeared extensively for other TV networks in the UK and America.

THE TRUE STORY OF THE SOLDIER PRINCE

HARRY'S WAR

ROBERT JOBSON

JOHN BLAKE

Published by John Blake Publishing Ltd,
3 Bramber Court, 2 Bramber Road,
London W14 9PB, UK

www.blake.co.uk

First published in paperback in 2008

ISBN: 978-1-84454-672-5

British Library Cataloguing-in-Publication Data:
A catalogue record for this book is available from the British Library.

Design by www.envydesign.co.uk

Printed and bound in Great Britain by Creative Print & Design,
Blaina, Wales

1 3 5 7 9 10 8 6 4 2

Text copyright © Robert Jobson, 2008

Photography courtesy of Empics/PA Photos and Getty Images/Tim Graham

Papers used by John Blake Publishing are natural, recyclable products
made from wood grown in sustainable forests. The manufacturing processes
conform to the environmental regulations of the country of origin.

In memory of Thomas Henry Albert Jobson (1911–1980)
Second World War Royal Navy veteran

CONTENTS

Acknowledgements   xi
Prologue   xiii
Chapter 1: An Officer and a Gentleman   1
Chapter 2: Baby Wales   13
Chapter 3: Fun and Young   29
Chapter 4: Boy Soldier   49
Chapter 5: Goodbye, Mummy   63
Chapter 6: Eton Rifles   73
Chapter 7: School's Out   91
Chapter 8: Harry the Nazi?   109
Chapter 9: Officer Cadet Wales   121
Chapter 10: Banned from Iraq   133
Chapter 11: I'm No Quitter   147
Chapter 12: Widow Six Seven   161
Chapter 13: Frontline Soldier   173
Chapter 14: In the Heat of the Battle   187
Chapter 15: Desert Morning Song   197
Chapter 16: Coming Home   209
Chapter 17: War is Over   221
Chapter 18: Real Heroes   231
Postscript   243

ACKNOWLEDGEMENTS

This book is written with the British servicemen and women who are serving our country in conflict areas around the world in mind. Prince Harry is just one of them. He has said he is no hero and publicly acknowledged that, as a British officer, he is just one of the tens of thousands of brave men and women who have put their lives on the line for Queen and country. All of us in Great Britain are indebted to them, whether we agree with the wars they are involved with or not.

This book tells the story of Prince Harry's fight to fulfil his ambition to serve his Queen and country on the frontline. Despite his privileged background, it was a long, hard fight. He lost his beloved mother, Diana, Princess of Wales, suddenly in a car accident, yet, despite that tragedy, he relentlessly pursued his dream to serve his country as a soldier. In serving on the frontline, Harry highlighted the risks being undertaken daily by our servicemen and women defending freedom in Afghanistan. He also risked his own life – showing true bravery by going to the frontline despite real threats from the Taliban and passionate supporters of Osama bin Laden that he would be specifically targeted and assassinated if located. He admitted being 'shit scared' – but he faced his fears and showed real courage by doing his duty.

I would like to thank my publisher, John Blake, for supporting me and the project – our second book together. I wish to thank my editor, Stuart Robertson, too, and the rest of the Blake team for all their hard work in producing this book at rapid speed. I am also indebted to Michael Leese for his help with the manuscript and his support. I would also like to thank my good friend Ken Wharfe MVO (Harry's Scotland Yard protection officer), Ian Walker, Patrick Jephson LVO, Dickie Arbiter LVO, Arthur Edwards MVO, Colleen Harris MVO, John Bingham, Mary Bull and HP for their help with the project.

Above all, I would like to thank Camilla, Alexandra and Charlie for their love and support and for just being there for me when I needed them.

PROLOGUE

'Dulce et decorum est pro patria mori'
(*It is sweet and fitting to die for one's country*)
WILFRED OWEN, WORLD WAR ONE SOLDIER-POET

It was just after 9 a.m. in early January 2008 as a young British army officer shaded his eyes and stared out over forbidding landscape. The sun was already high and a haze covered the fine dust of the Helmand desert that stretched out before him. He had rolled out of his cot a couple of hours earlier, pulled on his uniform and set off to catch up on what had been happening overnight. Then, under orders, he had headed for his position, always supported by his fellow soldiers. Eventually, he reached the designated location and stopped for a few moments to catch his breath. This was to be the moment he realised his life ambition.

Just 500 metres away across no-man's-land lay the heavily armed enemy – religious warriors fanatically supporting the Taliban cause and more than willing to die for it. But they were also skilled soldiers and would not just throw away their lives in a reckless assault. Cleverly, they kept themselves concealed, crouching out of sight. This was a bloody war of attrition and the enemy, despite devastating losses over years of fighting, just kept on coming. In many respects the skills of the Taliban soldiers, passed down from father to son, gave these fierce and driven fighting men an important advantage – something that had been drummed into the young officer at every stage of his training. This bleak terrain was, after all, their land. It was, they believed, no place for armed Western strangers in uniform who violated not only their home but their beliefs.

The moonscape of dirty orange rock and desert the British officer surveyed had been endlessly ravaged by war – too many years of bloody battle. From the days of Alexander the Great and Genghis Khan, blood had spilled and soaked into the sand and dust. In later times, soldiers of the British Raj had done their best to impose control on the region, and failed.

Pessimists recalled the grim reality of the retreat from Kabul 166 years earlier. Of the 16,500 officers and men who set off, only a handful made it back to base in Jalalabad alive to tell the awful tale.

The might of the Red Army of the once powerful Soviet Union had come unstuck here, too, when, 150 years or so later, they tried to impose their will on Afghanistan. The soldiers of both empires eventually had to concede defeat and were forced to withdraw. Although the tribes of this land clashed with each other, they were united in their hatred of outsiders. The Soviets had been embarrassingly driven back by determined fighters using weapons purchased with American money. It had been their

Vietnam. Now, ironically, the Americans, supported by their loyal British allies, were back fighting an enemy in the Taliban that their money and policies had helped create when the Cold War was at its height and the primary concern of the then President Reagan. Ever since 9/11, under the Bush administration the world had become a more complex place. There was no Soviet red bear for the West to hate, just an unseen enemy that operated in the shadows. America's new enemy was the religious warrior Osama bin Laden and his al-Qaeda network, a man whose myth and legend had been born of fighting in the mountains of Afghanistan.

The local Pashtuns, the indigenous tribe of southern Afghanistan and the largest ethnic group in the country, are a proud race. They are proud of their families and their country. They have a long and honourable tradition and are mentioned in ancient Aryan texts as the Paktua. The British called them Pathans, while they have often simply called themselves Afghans. They claim to be descended from Qais, a companion of the Islamic prophet Mohammed, and their evolved culture is naturally warm and welcoming to strangers. Those who completed the hippie trail in the Sixties will vouch for that. They have always prided themselves on giving the best available food to visitors. But in the first decade of the twenty-first century there is little chance of that. Now, the new 'strangers' in this province are battle-hardened frontline soldiers on both sides, and the extreme politics and violence that have consumed this area mean only those engaged in killing or saving lives get involved.

The young officer had read up on the proud Pashtun warriors. His father had always taught him to try to understand people of different race and origin and never to make snap judgements. He had listened but not always agreed. Others he trusted had at least advised him to know his enemy. His commanding officers had given him, and his brother officers, more specific instructions, as is the army's wont. But since he had arrived in Helmand, a place that resembled a *Mad Max* film, he had drawn his own conclusions. He was clear on how to deal with the locals. The advice from experienced soldiers on the ground was indelibly imprinted on his mind. They had told him to respect 'Terry Taliban', and he did. First and foremost a British soldier, he knew how to follow orders and to respect his instincts.

Frontline Afghanistan, the young officer knew, was no place for sentiment. There is no time to dwell on the beauty of the words of Khushal Khan Khattack, the Pashtun warrior-poet revered by the locals, much as Wilfred Owen, a soldier-poet and victim of World War One, is in the West. This was real war and the young officer knew it was a deadly business. Facing him was no ragtag army but an increasingly sophisticated Taliban force using al-Qaeda-inspired tactics that had been honed in the seemingly endless conflict in Iraq.

As the officer studied the terrain that lay ahead of him with a mixture of elation and trepidation, he knew only too well that he was going to have to draw on every scrap of expertise gained through the long hours of training at Sandhurst Military Academy and on exercises with his regiment, the Blues and Royals, back home. This he knew was no training exercise. He took steady, calming breaths, reassured by the knowledge that, while the enemy was good, his side was better – better trained, better equipped, better soldiers. But were they truly better soldiers? Did they know the inhospitable land as well as their enemy? That nagging doubt kept him alive to the real danger that faced him and his brothers-in-arms.

Then, slowly but surely Second Lieutenant Harry Wales, carefully placed both hands on the powerful .50-calibre machine gun in front of him. He paused for a heartbeat, then gently squeezed the trigger to send a stream of bullets hurtling towards the Taliban's defensive positions. This was the soldier-prince, at last free to do what he had wanted and play his role in the fight against terror. Like his royal ancestors at battles ranging from Agincourt to the Falklands, Prince Harry was willing to put his life on the line for Queen and country and to achieve his dreams. The location for the firefight was in the southernmost British position in Helmand. He was among a unit of battle-hardened Gurkhas repelling a ferocious attack by the insurgents.

The soldier-prince was carefully balanced on sandbags and made sure an open box of ammunition was close at hand as he took aim at the distant targets in front of him. Apart from the crash of weapons being fired, he had only distant puffs of smoke as the bullets hit the ground to guide his aim. As a fully trained battlefield air controller, Prince Harry was assigned a forward position on JTAC (Joint Tactical Air Coordination) Hill. Because it was so close to the Taliban trenches the hill was heavily defended but the men on it, including the prince, knew they were highly vulnerable to swift enemy action.

Suddenly, a force of as many as twenty Taliban fighters were spotted as they stealthily moved into position to launch an attack. With the alarm raised, the Gurkhas fired a Javelin missile at the attackers, which streaked towards them. Then came the order to man the machine guns and now it was Harry's turn to take part in his first action, just three weeks after arriving in Afghanistan. With his heart pumping, the twenty-three-year-old grandson of Queen Elizabeth II, his ultimate commander in chief as the British monarch, gritted his teeth as he surveyed his target.

With his earplugs carefully inserted to protect his hearing, Harry cheerfully admitted, 'This is the first time I've fired a .50 cal. It's just no-man's-land ...they poke their heads up and that's it.'

The prince's extraordinary introduction to live action was captured by a Gurkha soldier who filmed the moment on Harry's own camera. The half-kilometre-distant target had been dubbed 'Line Taunton', the heavily fortified trench system marking the start of a Taliban-controlled area extending as far south as the Pakistani border.

'The whole place is just deserted. There are no roofs on any of the compounds; there are craters all over the place; it looks like something out of the Battle of the Somme,' he remarked. Harry's immediate boss was Major Mark Milford, officer commanding of B Company of the 1st Battalion of the Royal Gurkha Rifles. 'This is the southern border for the coalition troops; this is about as dangerous as it can get,' he said.

As part of the same deployment, Harry went on patrol through the nearby bombed-out streets of Garmsir. Before his arrival in Afghanistan many had questioned whether he would ever get out on patrol because of the risk of his being recognised by the insurgents. The prince described the experience: 'Just walking around, some of the locals or the ANP [Afghan National Police] – they haven't got a clue who I am, they wouldn't know.'

The region had changed hands between Taliban and Coalition control several times, evidence of destruction is everywhere. But it is exactly this type of patrol that the army feels is vital to help it maintain control of the area. As someone recognised almost everywhere he has ever been in life, Harry found the anonymity clearly refreshing.

'It's fantastic,' Harry said in a Press Association interview. 'I'm still a little bit conscious [not to] show my face too much in and around the area. Luckily, there's no civilians around here ...it's sort of a little no-man's-land.'

Harry's induction to the frontline had begun a few weeks earlier on Christmas Day, and it was as far removed from the comforts of the Royal Family's Sandringham gathering as could be imagined. There were no presents and no sign of the lavish spread that would have been laid out for other members of his family. His Christmas was spent in a bullet-ridden madrasa (Islamic school) that had previously been home to the Taliban. It would be fair to describe conditions as Spartan, an uncomfortable camp bed for sleeping and washing outdoors in icy conditions.

At least he was able to tuck into one of the scrawny chickens that his Gurkha troops had slaughtered with their *kukris* (large knives). In conditions of utmost secrecy, with the British media promising to keep the information safe, Harry flew out to Afghanistan in mid-December. Within days of arriving at the isolated Forward Operating Base (FOB) Dwyer, headquarters of the battle group headed by his own Household Cavalry Regiment, the young prince was badgering his commanding officer, Colonel Edward Smyth-Osbourne, to be allowed to spend Christmas Day itself with the Gurkhas at FOB Delhi 11 kilometres away.

'I was hoping to come down here for Christmas Day to

be with the Gurkhas,' he explained. 'I don't know why, it was just something I wanted to do, just to be with them. They don't really celebrate Christmas that much but we had some fantastic games, which we played in the yard there,' he said at the time. 'I got nothing for Christmas; most of these guys got nothing for Christmas,' he said with a shrug.

As is the case in all British bases in Afghanistan, Second Lieutenant Wales enjoyed an alcohol-free holiday but was able to relieve tension with a series of raucous games with the Gurkhas, including one involving catching a chicken in the yard. The one concession to Christmas was an extra ten minutes' credit on his army satellite phone account over the Christmas week, in common with all the British troops. There were no concessions for his royal status and nor should there have been. He was in the army now, where he was just one of the men, and it was just how he liked it.

CHAPTER ONE

AN OFFICER AND A GENTLEMAN

'She was our guardian, friend and protector ...
quite simply the best mother in the world.'
PRINCE HARRY, 31 AUGUST 2007

I t was a defining moment in Harry Wales's young life, the moment Princess Diana's second son finally came of age. Perhaps it was fitting, too that, a decade after her tragic death the memory of his mother had forced this sometimes wayward young man to begin shedding his adolescent playboy image at last. Perhaps, too, given his personal history, it should have come as no surprise that he wanted to kick out and rebel against those who advised him that his status dictated that he had to conform. After all, hadn't they told his mother the same thing?

The tall, flame-haired twenty-two-year-old showed no sign of nerves as he stood to deliver what was to be a brilliant tribute to Diana. Also present and watching him were those who had been closest to her throughout her short life. They were gathered at the Guards' Chapel, Wellington Barracks, in central London for a special service to mark exactly a decade since her untimely passing in a car crash in a Parisian tunnel.

At the rehearsal the previous day, Harry admitted to feeling really nervous about delivering the address. But when it came to the real thing he stood tall and proud before a congregation of almost five hundred people – including his grandmother the Queen, his father the Prince of Wales, his grandfather the Duke of Edinburgh and the newly installed British Prime Minister Gordon Brown – as well as a global television audience of millions.

I stood opposite Buckingham Palace a few hundred yards from the chapel where Princes William and Harry had greeted their guests with warmth and welcoming smiles. Commentating for the global news network CNN with my friend the irrepressible Richard Quest, I was struck by the sureness of Diana's sons. This was something they clearly both wanted, even if their grandmother, their father and certainly their stepmother, the Duchess of Cornwall (formerly Camilla Parker Bowles), were of the view that it would have been better if no service of thanksgiving had taken place.

Inevitably, the media focus had been on Camilla's decision not to attend the service despite her initial acceptance of the princes' invitation. Like the tough newsman he is, Richard addressed the issue as soon as we were on air. CNN was not in the business of sentiment, just news.

'Camilla's invitation to attend the service came from Princes William and Harry themselves,' Richard began, introducing a lengthy opening line. 'They have a close relationship with their stepmother and they wanted her to be there. But, in a statement from Clarence House,

Camilla said her attendance would divert attention from the purpose of the occasion, which was to focus on the life and service of Diana. And so she would withdraw. Camilla is probably right in assuming that the focus of attention would have been on her. After all, this is the woman who has always been at the centre of the breakdown of Diana's marriage.'

I could not help but agree, and chipped in with, 'Up to 70 per cent of the people of this country thought it was wrong that Camilla should be there. She was seen as the person that broke up this marriage, rightly or wrongly. And the fact is it was going to be all about Camilla and not about Diana, and that in my opinion would have been wrong.'

It was just what the Queen and the Royal Family did not want to hear. A decade after her sudden death in a car accident in a Paris road tunnel, Diana still haunted the woman destined to reign alongside King Charles III, should he ever ascend the throne and take that title. The Duchess of Cornwall as ever had done her best to defuse the situation as much for Charles's sake as her own. She issued a dignified statement through the Press Association, saying that she was 'very touched' to have been invited. 'I accepted and wanted to support them; however, on reflection, I believe my attendance could divert attention from the purpose of the occasion, which is to focus on the life and service of Diana. I'm grateful to my husband, William and Harry for supporting my decision.'

Her announcement came just hours after a column written by one of Diana's best friends, the Honourable Rosa Monckton, had published an op-ed in the *Daily Mail*, the princess's favourite newspaper, rightly pointing out that the princess would have been 'astonished' if Camilla were there. She wrote,

> Now controversy surrounds the very service designed to give thanks for her life. And so, once again, I feel I should go in to bat on her behalf. Can you imagine if she had actually shown up? This is a woman that Diana had called the 'third person' in her marriage with Prince Charles. All of our families have strained relationships that rise to the surface at weddings, funerals and other events. But this is arguably the most public family in the world, and everyone knows what happened between Diana, Charles and Camilla. Instead, Prince Charles angered a lot of people, and it's left to Prince William and Prince Harry to try to smooth things over with their grace and humility – two traits they inherited from their mother.

After that forthright statement by a woman still perceived as the keeper of Diana's flame, there was no way Camilla could attend even if Charles had begged her to. It was not surprising, then, that, when Charles arrived at the chapel entrance to be greeted with affectionate kisses from his sons, his demeanour, no matter how hard he tried to shield his true feelings, looked uneasy. He looked a little lost without Camilla, the second wife he had fought so hard to be publicly accepted at his side and once again had been thwarted by the ghost of his first wife.

But this day was not about Charles. It was the chance for Diana's 'boys' to thank the woman stripped of her royal title to be remembered and for her family, friends and admirers to thank God for her life. For so long in the years since their mother's passing, Harry and his older brother William had been referred to by officials and the media commentators alike as 'the boys'. But on that day, that special day of remembrance, her second son Harry was a boy no longer. He emerged from it as a confident, strapping young man, and a man ready to defend his mother's memory and his family honour from all those he and his brother felt had hijacked it.

Unfazed by the enormity of the moment, Harry spoke from the heart and with real passion of his mother's 'unrivalled love of life, laughter, fun and folly'. 'She was our guardian, friend and protector,' he said, as his older brother, with whom he had organised the service, looked on. 'She never once allowed her unfaltering love for us to go unspoken or undemonstrated.

'She will always be remembered for her amazing public work. But behind the media glare, to us, just two loving children, she was quite simply the best mother in the world.'

It was brilliant, rousing stuff and as Harry talked he began to relax; there was even a hint of smile, before he added, 'We would say that, wouldn't we? But we miss her. Put simply, she made us and so many other people happy. May this be the way that she is remembered.'

It was moving without lapsing into the sentimental. Inevitably, it drew tears as well as spontaneous applause from the loyal Diana fans gathered outside the chapel behind barriers. The simplicity of his words and eloquence touched a chord with those watching on television, perhaps surprised to see such a mature performance from a young man with a louche reputation. The echoes from a decade earlier, when his uncle, Earl Spencer, embittered and passionate, delivered his biting eulogy to his dead sister were obvious. But this time there was no malice in his tribute, nor any nervous glances or discomfort from those present to hear it.

This was a clear attempt by Diana's sons – William assisted with the writing of the speech – to show the world that they had learned to smile through the pain and were now intent on celebrating their mother's remarkable life, her gifts and achievements rather than dwell on the manner of her death and the almost never-ending – and increasingly fanciful – conspiracy theories attached to her name.

Clarence House officials gave no official explanation as to why it fell to Harry to give the address rather than his older brother. Physically, William is the one who more closely resembles his mother and is often perceived as the standard bearer of Diana's legacy. Perhaps it was thought Harry would be better at it. And nobody could argue against that logic. For, on the rare occasions the princes have spoken together in public, such as at the Diana memorial concert at Wembley Stadium, Harry always appeared the more relaxed and self-assured. Perhaps – not hampered by the pressure of one day getting the top job – Harry is freer to express himself in public.

During the downtime of the live broadcast, as Richard Quest busied himself skimming through his exhaustive research notes in readiness for the next live link with CNN in the Atlanta headquarters, my mind drifted back to the day of Diana's funeral at Westminster Abbey, which I had attended in my capacity as a journalist. The funeral had taken place just a few hundred yards away from where we had gathered for her memorial service. Back then, the tiny figure of Harry, at the time just shy of his thirteenth birthday, his fists tightly clenched with emotion, walked behind his mother's coffin biting his lip. That day he was flanked by his father, uncle, grandfather and brother for support, but he was the focus to many, because he was so much smaller than the others and seemed much more vulnerable. Even his fifteen-year-old brother stood shoulder to shoulder with the adults. Nothing any of the weeping mourners felt that day could be eclipsed by the pain felt by her two young sons.

Ten years on, Harry's dignity moved some to weep again, but this time it was the eloquence of his speech that led to the tears, not his broken vulnerability. William, then twenty-five, sat in the front pew next to the Queen as Harry spoke and listened intently. He knew every word that Harry would say and he agreed with every one of them, nodding occasionally as his brother spoke. Just moments before Harry had got to his feet, William had delivered his own reading from the Bible, from St Paul's letter to the Ephesians, biting his lip at one point as he paused between sentences. He knew he had to hold himself. He would one day be King and he had to be strong in public.

William and Harry had entered the chapel with their father, the Prince of Wales, the Queen, dressed in vivid purple, and Prince Philip. The young princes had walked slowly up the aisle to the strains of 'The Londonderry Air', passing the Prime Minister and some of his predecessors, celebrity guests including Cliff Richard and Elton John, and friends and associates from the public and private life of the princess.

The service was conducted by the Reverend Patrick Irwin, chaplain to the Household Division, and included two prayers written for the occasion by Dr Rowan Williams, the Archbishop of Canterbury, at the request of William and Harry. William, as the future King, sat with the Windsors. Prince Harry sat with the Spencers in a pointed and public show of unity between the two families.

The Bishop of London, a close friend of the Prince of Wales, delivered the eulogy in the sixty-minute service and said that it should mark the moment 'we let Diana rest in peace'. He said, 'It is easy to lose the real person in the image, to insist that all is darkness or all is light. Still, ten years after her tragic death, there are regular reports of "fury" at this or that incident and the princess's memory is used for scoring points. Let it end here.

'Let this service mark the point at which we let her rest in peace and dwell on her memory with thanksgiving and compassion,' he said. Her sons nodded in agreement.

But there was little chance of that. The Harrods owner and tycoon Mohamed al-Fayed's legal team were busying themselves pursuing conspiracy theories ahead of the inquests into the deaths of Princess Diana and her last boyfriend Dodi Fayed, al-Fayed's eldest son, which were to be heard before the coroner, Lord Justice Scott Baker, in London that autumn.

At those hearings, which lasted until April 2008, Diana's life and the alleged reasons for her death would be examined for public consumption in forensic detail. It was deeply personal and at times offensive to her memory and those of her family. Details of a conversation between Diana and her mother, Frances Shand Kydd, during which the latter allegedly called her a 'whore' for her involvement with Muslim men, were revealed. Even highly personal information about her menstrual cycle and use of contraception had been openly discussed at the inquest, held at the Royal Courts of Justice.

But to what end? One could forgive Diana's sons for questioning the necessity or relevance of such claims by the man who was described as fantasist, the so-called 'rock' and keeper of secrets, the princess's ex-butler Paul Burrell. Surely, she should have been allowed dignity in death.

Indeed, in the early months of 2008, it was as if the princess had never died, as every last detail of her life was splashed across the national newspapers in Britain, and television networks in America and around the world broadcast them relentlessly. Her sons' attempt to grab hold of their mother's legacy seemed, at least in the short term, to have failed.

For William and Harry, the music – played by the orchestra from the Royal Academy of Music, of which Diana was the president – was especially evocative of life with their mother. They made their choices after listening to the music on their iPods and texting each other. Diana used to play them Rachmaninov's 'Vespers' on car journeys. The princes chose the Guards' Chapel because it was the closest to a mother church for their regiment, the Household Cavalry. Both wore their regimental ties. It is also a short walk from Buckingham Palace, where, back in July 1981, as a young bride, their mother kissed the Prince of Wales on the balcony in front of adoring crowds who were to follow her for the rest of her short life.

Diana's siblings, Earl Spencer, Lady Sarah McCorquodale and Lady Jane Fellowes, who helped

William and Harry with arrangements, were there with the rest of the Spencer relatives. Two Welsh Guards, in their distinctive red tunics, stood guard outside the chapel. It was an emotional journey for them, too. Colour Sergeant Carl Taylor and Lance Sergeant Chris Traherne were pallbearers at Diana's funeral. The service ended with 'I Vow To Thee, My Country', which was Diana's favourite hymn. She chose it for her wedding in St Paul's Cathedral – the hymn was played again at her funeral. As the National Anthem began, the sun began to shine for the first time.

Diana's admirers, many of them still suspicious of the cause of her death, had tied bouquets, poems and portraits to the gates of her former home at Kensington Palace. Flowers piled up, too, at Althorp, Diana's childhood home and final resting place, which broke with tradition by opening to the public for the anniversary. In Paris, above the Pont de l'Alma tunnel, where Diana's fatal accident occurred, dozens of well-wishers from around the world came with flowers and candles. They left messages on the Flame of Liberty, a gilded torch statue built in 1987 to celebrate Franco-American friendship but adopted by Diana mourners straight after her death.

Harry was pleased the service had gone so well – winning over some of those who questioned whether it should have happened in the first place. The army – it seemed then – may have denied the soldier-prince his chance to go into battle, but his courage before a global audience rightly won him widespread respect. That day Harry, a second lieutenant (or cornet) in the Blues and Royals, showed his real colours, and at last emerged from the shadows cast by his late mother and older brother. Perhaps for the first time since he had walked, head bowed, behind his mother's coffin as a waif, a broken boy, Harry registered on the world stage – and for all the right reasons. This time he stood on that stage as an officer, a gentleman and a soldier-prince – and his late mother would have undoubtedly been proud.

CHAPTER TWO

BABY WALES

'Oh, it's a boy ... and it's even got red hair.'
PRINCE CHARLES'S ALLEGED REMARK TO DIANA MOMENTS
AFTER HARRY'S BIRTH

Prince Charles had stayed at his wife's side throughout her exhausting nine-hour labour. He had given her ice cubes to suck when she was thirsty and held her hand in support and encouraged her, although he later admitted to dozing off a couple of times. Diana finally gave birth to a second son at 4.20 p.m. on Saturday, 15 September 1984, in the Lindo Wing of St Mary's Hospital, Paddington. 'Baby Wales', as he was called then, weighed 6 pounds 14 ounces and had red hair. It should have been one of the proudest moments in the lives of the Prince and Princess of Wales. The birth of William meant the House of Windsor had a healthy heir; now the Royal Family had its 'spare to the heir' and the line of succession was secured. Moments after the birth, so the story goes, the couple's happiness was shattered when in a moment of thoughtlessness, or worse, Charles made an unforgivable remark to his tired and emotional young wife. According to Diana he turned to her on seeing his baby son and said, 'Oh, it's a boy ... and it's even got red hair.'

Many people since have read too much into this. Some claim, with the benefit of hindsight, that Charles may have been casting some doubt over Harry's paternity. The reason for this is that the Cavalry officer Major James Hewitt, whom the princess publicly admitted to having 'loved and adored', had red hair too. The fact that at this time Diana and Major Hewitt had not yet met seems to have escaped them.

It was simpler than that. Charles knew that red hair was a Spencer trait. The comment hurt Diana. Much later, she said rather dramatically that his comments marked the beginning of the end of their marriage. Justifiably, Diana was infuriated by what she interpreted as Charles's dismissive, even cruel, comments about their new baby.

Something inside her died.

Until that point she claimed she had harboured real hopes that, despite obvious problems in their marriage, a new baby would bring them closer together. There had been moments of shared intimacy between the births of William in 1982 and Harry two years later. But the relationship lacked passion, which even the sexually naïve Diana thought odd. Charles had stopped sleeping with her and their sex life was virtually nonexistent by then.

The princess, at just twenty-four, felt lost and abandoned by the only lover she had ever known. The princess later revealed her thoughts to the actor Peter Settelen, her voice coach, in a series of taped interviews he later sold to NBC news network long after her death.

He asked, 'There's virtually no sexual relations between you two?' She replied frankly, 'Well, there was, it was there, it was there and then it fizzled out about seven years ago ... Well, seven was Harry. It was eight ...' Asked how she knew it was odd, Diana replied, 'Instinct told me. It was just so odd. I just don't know. There was never a requirement for it from [sic] his case. Sort of once every three weeks, and I kept thinking, and then I followed a pattern: he used to see his lady once every three weeks before we got married ...'

But it was not just Diana who felt lost. In the year before Harry's birth, Charles too felt trapped in a marriage with a woman with whom he felt he had little in common. At this time the couple tried to put on a brave face, and lunched powerful media figures in a charm offensive. After one lunch with the couple the editor of the *Sunday Times*, Andrew Neil, concluded that they had little in common. He recalled how Charles 'roamed far and wide on the issues of the day' but he made no attempt to involve his wife in the conversation, who said very little at the meeting at Kensington Palace, also attended by Diana's first cousin, Charles Douglas-Home, then editor of Neil's sister newspaper, *The Times*. Charles knew then that there were serious problems in his relationship and confided to a friend, 'How awful incompatibility is, and how dreadfully destructive it can be for the players in this extraordinary drama! It has all the ingredients of a Greek tragedy.' It was typically melodramatic of a man who has always seen himself as an academic, despite his average performance as an undergraduate.

The prince's barbed 'red hair' comments are now recorded in history and widely believed. But some well-placed figures now seriously doubt that he ever made them. They go further and insist the prince was 'overjoyed' at the birth of his second son had expressed as much to the princess. Whatever the truth, the alleged comments, which first appeared in Andrew Morton's biography *Diana: Her True Story*, stuck. It was a devastating book that the princess both inspired and colluded in with the help of her friend and intermediary Dr James Coldhurst. It was written years after Harry's birth, and in the first edition the word 'red' was not used by Morton, who quoted Charles as saying 'rusty hair' instead.

At the time, Diana publicly denied having had anything to do with the book. She even perpetuated the lie to the Queen. 'I have never met him [Andrew Morton],' she told Sir Robert Fellowes, her brother-in-law and then the Queen's private secretary, her most senior aide. Of course, it proved one of Diana's boldest lies. She had met him in his capacity as a royal reporter on tours. In truth, she had inspired and practically written the book. She may have not met him directly, using intermediary James Coldhurst to get the tapes to the author, but she had clearly lied to her mother-in-law and monarch. It was a lie that finally sounded the death knell on the royal marriage and ended any chance of her ever becoming Queen. How could anyone ever trust her again? While it was brilliant journalism, Andrew Morton's book was effectively the longest, most celebrated and one-sided divorce petition in history. Charles was 'exposed' as a cruel, heartless adulterer; Diana as a heroic, almost faultless victim, almost saintly.

Many close to the prince to this day strenuously deny he ever made such thoughtless comments; and remember things very differently. They insist the prince was 'absolutely thrilled' to witness the birth, and definitely made no malicious comment about Harry's hair (which was at the time more blond than red). It was part of Diana's 'preposterous' spin planned years later and designed to destroy her husband's credibility. Indeed, they say that by the time she conveniently 'remembered' his remarks, Diana had grown to despise Charles for rejecting her in favour of his previous lover Camilla Parker Bowles. 'What kind of parent is it who publicly accuses her son's father of not really wanting him? It was downright shameful,' a member of the prince's staff later told me. One could not help but agree.

Whatever the truth about Charles's comments 'Baby Wales' was undoubtedly born into the heart of a serious family crisis. The colour of his hair was the tip of the iceberg. After all, it could not have come as much of a surprise, especially since it was a Spencer family trait. Diana's sister Lady Sarah McCorquodale had the same colouring, as did half of those featured in the portraits of Spencer ancestors hanging on the walls of Althorp. One was even known as the 'Red Earl' (1835–1910), who boasted a bright, rusty orange beard to match his locks.

By this time, autumn of 1984, Diana simply did not trust her husband and, with hindsight, probably with good reason. She was convinced in the months before Harry's birth that Camilla Parker Bowles, his one-time married lover, was back in his life. Despite his reassurances, she simply did not believe him. She was heartbroken by the overt betrayal. In the months leading up to the birth, Diana had truly harboured romantic hopes that at last her marriage could realise her dreams, despite the difficulties the couple had experienced. She had hoped that their second child would bring her and Charles closer together as a couple. The birth of a baby might even save it, she told friends. But it was to prove a vain hope.

Ironically, the six weeks before the birth had, according to the princess, been the happiest period of their married life. She described the balmy summer of 1984 as a 'time of contentment and mutual devotion'. But, sadly, it was not to last, and storm clouds were gathering overhead. The fairytale marriage that had promised so much at its inception was already doomed.

Harry had been conceived at Sandringham, the Queen's country estate in Norfolk in the east of England – as 'if by a miracle', Diana said. Many years later she confided to her Scotland Yard personal protection officer, Inspector Ken Wharfe, 'I don't know how my husband and I did have Harry because by then he had gone back to his lady, but one thing that is absolutely certain is that we did.'

Ahead of the official announcement of the pregnancy by Buckingham Palace, Diana flew to Norway on her first official solo tour. When she got back she found a tender love note from her husband. It read, 'We are so proud of you.' Charles had signed it, 'Willie the Wombat and I'. It was a thoughtful gesture, but for all its good intentions it failed to lift the spirits of the by now increasingly temperamental princess, whose violent mood swings were beginning to cause growing concern in the corridors of the palace.

To be fair Diana's pregnancy was not easy. She suffered from morning sickness and by that stage in her young life had been diagnosed with the eating disorder bulimia. Overwrought and tired, she had to endure many sleepless nights attending to William, who was teething at the time. It prompted the princess to utter the line a few months into the pregnancy, 'I've not felt well since day one. I don't think I'm made for the production of babies ...' She added, 'If men had babies, they would only have once each.'

The reality of her situation was hard to bear. Barely three years into their marriage, both Charles and Diana had begun to realise that they were poles apart emotionally, mentally and physically, and not even another child could fill the gaping void. All his life Charles, indulged as only the heir to a throne can be, had been used to getting his own way and following his own path. In adulthood, too, he had thoroughly enjoyed his bachelor existence, and he did not seem to appreciate that married life may curtail that freedom.

Diana, an emotional soul, began to question his every move. But among her nagging doubts she still harboured one hope – perhaps the new baby would give them a fresh start. Charles was enthusiastic at first. He cherished the idea of having a little girl. But Diana knew from a hospital scan that she was expecting another son. She had kept the news from him, knowing that he would be disappointed. It was a secret she nursed right up until the moment that Harry was born. Whatever the sex of the child, it could hardly have saved a marriage set on a collision course, racked with guilt, adultery and incompatibility.

It was not until nearly a decade later, in June 1994, that Charles finally admitted adultery during the course of a two-and-a-half-hour documentary meant to champion him, but even then he ducked the specifics. Three-quarters of the way through Jonathan Dimbleby's sympathetic portrayal, the prince – sitting stiffly on a chintz-covered sofa – was asked point-blank by Dimbleby if he had tried to be 'faithful and honourable' when he married Diana.

'Yes, absolutely,' the then forty-five-year-old prince replied.

'And you were?' pressed Dimbleby.

'Yes.' Then, after a pregnant pause, he added, 'Until it became irretrievably broken down, us both having tried.'

Dimbleby – who also penned a comprehensive biography of the prince, *The Prince of Wales: A Biography*, in 1994 written with his cooperation – became a friend and confidant in the process. Many saw him as an apologist and perhaps his assertion that Charles did not rekindle his affair until November 1986 should be taken with this in mind. Another pro-Charles author, the former Oxford scholar and British Tory Member of Parliament Gyles Brandreth, put the date even later, at June 1987, in his book *Charles & Camilla: Portrait of a Love Affair*. He claimed that Charles took the fact that Diana danced provocatively with her former beau Philip Dunne in June, when at the wedding of Tracy Ward, and the Marquess of Worcester as evidence that she too was enjoying extramarital affairs. That, he thought, was a green light for him to pursue his own private life.

Others believe that for all Diana's bouts of paranoia she was right to suspect that the prince and Camilla were intimate even before the birth of his second son. But the precise detail of who was cheating on whom was an irrelevance. The point, surely, was that both felt the need to find solace with other partners from a very early point in their marriage, an act that would inevitably sound the death knell for any marriage, let alone one conducted in the public eye. But at this time it was a private trauma, for to the outside world Charles and Diana were the perfect married couple, and, as far as the Queen was concerned, they had secured the line of succession by producing an heir – and now, in Harry, the 'spare' – to the throne.

After the birth, at 6.35 p.m., Charles left the hospital and went back to the couple's London home Kensington Palace stating 'I need a drink,' before promptly downing his favourite, a large, stiff dry martini. He returned to the hospital the following day bringing William and the nanny, Barbara Barnes, with him. True to form, two-year-old William promptly caused a rumpus by running out of the lift giving his bodyguards the slip, if only for a few seconds. At one point, the protection officer barged into a hospital screen outside the princess's door and she went to look to see what was happening, to see her little boy running towards her. She scooped him into her arms and it was from there that he first clapped eyes on his little brother, who was swaddled in a white blanket. Excited, the future king rushed over and kissed Harry's forehead. Afterwards, he was even allowed to cradle the newborn prince in his arms, watched by his parents.

Diana resolved to leave the hospital as early as possible, as she had done with Prince William, and, at 2.30 p.m. the following day, she returned to Kensington Palace. To her annoyance, as soon as she returned home, Charles announced he was off to play polo at Windsor, leaving his wife alone with her children. Charles saw nothing wrong in his actions, but Diana again saw it as a sign of his thoughtlessness.

Blood royals do not always follow family convention. When the Queen and Prince Philip were told of the news of Harry's birth, they were out shooting in Scotland. They did not return to London until a week later and, while the

Queen did go to see her fourth grandson when she got back, Philip, who was always a law unto himself, went carriage-driving on his return and then jetted off to Canada. Asked about his grandson, the nonplussed Duke responded with, 'I haven't seen him yet – I've been too busy.' Several weeks later he finally relented and met his grandson for the first time. The reaction at Althorp was very different. Johnnie Spencer, Diana's affable father, literally put the flags out. He was thrilled and contacted the press saying his grandson was a 'fine chap'. He subsequently set up a trust fund worth millions for his grandson.

Charles was later to complain of his own father's rather offhand parenting; Diana felt he, too, was equally distant. Charles believed his father had no choice but to attend a longstanding commitment. He hated the idea of letting people down. Diana would often remind him later that such consideration did not seem to extend to her and their children. In public at least Charles was making all the right noises. At the polo match at Smith's Lawn the new father was presented with a magnum of champagne by Johnny Kidd, the dashing grandson of the great newspaper proprietor Lord Beaverbrook and captain of the opposing team. At the impromptu party that followed, Charles declared proudly, 'We nearly have a full polo team.' (A polo team has four players.)

But, despite the early euphoria, Harry's arrival certainly upset the rather spoiled toddler William. Until then he had been the focus of his parents' world as well as the centre of attention of the coterie of staff in their household. William, even at a tender age, loved the attention his status granted him. Diana noted that William revelled in the attention. He could not even fall over without a member of the

Kensington Palace staff rushing over and picking him up and dusting him down.

He was a hit with the public, too. Charles and Diana understood the thirst for information and pictures of the prince, and arranged a number of staged photocalls for the cameras and television. At eighteen months, he toddled out for the ''tographers', as he called them, in the walled garden of Kensington Palace. Six months later, he returned for the sequel to celebrate his second birthday, performing for the cameras again by kicking a football and blurting out 'Daddy' to his father's and the journalists' delight.

Harry's birth changed everything. The focus shifted to the rusty-haired baby, at least for a while. Diana was keen to prevent William's jealousy from getting out of hand and did everything she could to ensure that the two boys would bond. William was taken to the hospital to meet his little brother for the first time and organised for him to present him with a soft toy. 'William spends the entire time pouring an endless supply of hugs and kisses on Harry and we are hardly allowed near,' Diana said.

Nothing could stop William's jealousy. Charles felt it was only to be expected and urged his wife not to worry. The new father was also pleased that his younger son was less boisterous than William had been as a baby. He recalled that Harry was 'extraordinarily good, sleeps marvellously and eats well'. He also said that Harry was 'the one with the gentle nature'.

As Diana already knew the sex of her baby, she had been mulling over it for weeks. She had already made up her mind about his name. She stuck to her guns despite Prince Charles's preference for his son to be called Albert, after his grandfather (King George VI elected to be called George when king, despite having hitherto been called Albert, the first of his four given names). Eventually, he bowed to his wife to keep the peace. The gruff Canadian Vic Chapman, who was officially assistant press secretary to the Queen but in reality handled Charles and Diana, made the announcement from the steps of the Lindo Wing. The former football player took the unusual step of declaring to the waiting journalists, 'OK, the name is Prince Henry Charles Albert David. They intend to call him Prince Harry.'

Even after Harry's birth, Charles had apparently bemoaned the fact that he had another son, but this time he said it to the wrong person, for when he voiced this to Frances Shand Kydd, Diana's forthright mother, she snapped back, 'Just be grateful he's healthy.' From that moment on, Charles stopped going on about the daughter he never had, but his relations with his mother-in-law remained strained until the end. When she died aged sixty-eight in June 2004, Charles stayed away from her funeral on the Isle of Seil, Scotland, although his sons attended.

Four days before Christmas, there was another controversy, this time over Harry's christening. Diana's strained relationship with her sister-in-law, Princess Anne, caused more problems within 'the Firm'. Diana pointedly didn't ask Anne to become Harry's godmother at his christening, as was expected.

Prince Philip was said to be furious about the snub to his daughter. Anne, too, was said to be irritated. The palace statement insisted that Anne and her then husband Captain Mark Philips had a shooting party at Gatcombe and could not leave their guests. But it did little to dampen down the row, which spilled over into the media.

But the fact remains that he refused to confirm or deny

claims that he had been personally telephoned by Prince Charles over the original report by the official court correspondent, Grania Forbes. Some thought, perhaps rightly, that Chipp protested just a little too much.

Whatever the truth, the furore left the feeling that there was little love lost between the two women, and neither appeared to care who knew about it.

To show solidarity, Anne's children, Peter and Zara, did attend.

Another row soon followed over the first offering in his new role by the new Poet Laureate, Ted Hughes, of a poem purporting to be about the christening, just two days after his appointment. The role of Poet Laureate – its £70-a-year-and-a-case-of-wine salary – carries no official duties, but previous incumbents had written for state occasions. The unconventional Mr Hughes was strongly criticised by his peers, including the poet and novelist Kingsley Amis, who described the lengthy poem as long and boring. 'It really has very little to do with the subject. Unless we had been told, we would not connect it with the christening of Prince Harry,' he said. Amis concluded, 'It is a terrifically boring poem and very difficult to follow.'

Hughes escaped the row over his poem – which linked the blessings of a drought-breaking storm in Devon with the blessing of a baby prince and holy water – by going fishing in Ireland.

Thankfully, the ceremony itself – conducted by the Archbishop of Canterbury, Dr Robert Runcie, on 21 December in St George's Chapel, within the grounds of Windsor Castle – broke with royal tradition. Until then, most royal babies – including Harry's brother William – had been baptised in the Music Room at Buckingham

Palace. The three-month-old Harry cried for only two or three minutes while the archbishop performed the blessing with holy water. 'He was as quiet as a mouse throughout the rest,' said one of the choristers.

In another departure, the Queen agreed that, despite the fact that the event was a strictly family occasion, the entire nation could share it with television pictures being broadcast in her Christmas message a few days later. Despite the media rumpus, the christening went without a hitch.

Princess Margaret's daughter, Lady Sarah Armstrong-Jones, was asked to be godmother, along with Carolyn Bartholomew Diana's old flatmate, Lady Vestey. Harry's uncle the Duke of York, portrait painter Bryan Organ and Gerald Ward, an old friend of Prince Charles, were the three godfathers.

Harry was undoubtedly the star of the show. But afterwards it was his brother who stole a large slice of the limelight. William's antics and his infectious laughter as Lord Snowdon – Princess Margaret's ex-husband and photographer on the day – took the official portraits. All eyes were on William as he cheekily twizzled and turned in front of the group, causing the Queen and Prince Charles to burst out laughing. William, just two-and-a-half-years old and described by his father as a 'spindly little character with a good sense of humour', loved every minute of it. He was fascinated by a clockwork birdie in a cage given to him by Lord Snowdon while the pictures were taken.

Four generations of the Royal Family attended the baptism, and at the photo session that followed there was no mistaking the pride on the Queen Mother's face as the then eighty-five-year-old former Queen Consort took her fourth great-grandchild in her arms while he plucked at the christening robe of Honiton lace that had been used in royal baptisms since the days of the Empress Queen Victoria. Film footage of the christening and the party that followed was shown on Christmas Day in the Queen's broadcast. In it, William was seen galloping through the corridors of Windsor Castle and chasing round the Archbishop of Canterbury in a game of tag with his cousins, Peter and Zara Phillips.

Diana is heard explaining to William how many generations of the Royal Family had worn the robe that his little brother was wearing. 'Great-granny was christened in it,' she said before Charles jumped in with, 'And I was christened in it,' trying to cover-up his wife's mistake on film. (The Queen Mother was the daughter of the Earl of Strathmore and, although descended from Robert II, King of Scotland, in the fourteenth century had definitely not worn the royal robe at her baptism.)

William's excited behaviour and the happy smiling faces at the christening party delighted millions as they celebrated Christmas at home with their families in front of their television sets. But the public-relations masterstroke masked the truth. The on-screen royal smiles belied the painful truth of a 'fairytale' marriage in freefall and a royal family on the brink of a crisis that would rock the monarchy to its foundations.

CHAPTER THREE

FUN AND YOUNG

'My children are the most important things in my life.'
DIANA, PRINCESS OF WALES

Princess Diana agonised about the best way to raise her sons. She knew they had to be made aware of royal customs she regarded as stuffy and outmoded, but she wanted them to be free spirits just the same. She would spend hours locked in conversations with her older sister, Lady Jane Fellowes, who, like her, had married into the Royal Family system, albeit on a significantly lower scale. Jane had wed Sir Robert Fellowes, who rose to become the Queen's most trusted servant and served with distinction as her private secretary, one of the most senior positions in the royal household. Diana confided in Jane in the early days and asked for help about the best way to educate her sons and prepare them for the unique life experiences that lay before them.

Charles felt it was best to follow the tried and tested royal path of employing a governess, preferably one with experience of teaching members of the Royal Family. He and his mother had benefited form the closeted experience and he saw no reason why his sons should need anything different. Diana, however, was determined that it was not going to happen. Jane – whose children, Laura (born in 1980) and Alexander (three years later), also lived at Kensington Palace – and Diana were almost exact maternal contemporaries, and Jane agreed with Diana's thinking about how to raise the children. Diana believed William and Harry would benefit from mixing with what they termed 'ordinary' children. (Of course these 'ordinary' children would inevitably come from very privileged backgrounds of wealth and social status.)

Endless rows ensued, during which the princess made it clear to Prince Charles that she didn't want her sons locked in a schoolroom high in the house somewhere with only a few handpicked friends as playmates. She wanted them to grow freely and naturally among their peers. In her more vindictive moments, Diana reminded Charles that, just because he had been raised badly, it was wrong to inflict the mistakes of his parents on their children. She painfully reminded the prince that his childhood had left him an emotional wreck, withdrawn, socially inept and unable to cope with personal criticism. How could he argue with her? Eventually the shutters came down and his wilful wife won the day. After all, how could he bemoan his experiences, which he often did, and then insist his own children follow the same miserable route?

The princess was keen to send William to Young England kindergarten in Pimlico, central London, an upmarket nursery where she had worked after leaving finishing school. When she tried him out at the nursery she was upset by the fact that he failed to participate fully with the other children in the group, who all energetically joined in playing 'Galloping Horses', in which toddlers play at being horses. Diana was horrified when William appeared to be left out by the rest of the group. Perhaps overreacting, she saw his inability to interact as evidence of the need for decisive action. Diana cast around for somewhere nearer to send her older son, and eventually picked a small school run by a bishop's daughter, Mrs Jane Mynors, in a tree-lined street a few minutes' walk from Kensington Palace at Chepstow Villas in Notting Hill.

Not for the first time William blazed a trail for his younger brother; where William went Harry would inevitably follow.

Diana prided herself on her abilities as a mother. 'My children are the most important things in my life. I love them to death,' she confided. But in those early days Diana relied heavily on the wisdom and experience of Nanny Barbara Barnes.

Diana was adamant that her children were not going to experience the same kind of upbringing she did. She told friends that, as the product of a dysfunctional family, she was often left alone in her bed, frightened and confused about what was going on around her.

'A child's stability arises mainly from the affection received from their parents, and there is no substitute for affection,' she said when describing how she would always make sure that William and Harry came first.

When the boys went away to boarding school she pined for them and couldn't wait to receive letters from them and wrote to them twice a week.

Despite marrying into the Royal Family, with all its rank

and privilege, she was determined that when it came to her own children she would have her own way.

Like many from broken homes, she did her best to give her sons as secure an environment as possible. Fortunately, this was one area where Prince Charles truly respected her beliefs. Charles was pretty much old-school when it came to motherhood and the duties of his wife. Although society's attitude has changed concerning the role of women, Charles believes one of the most important roles any woman can ever perform is to be a mother. 'Nobody should denigrate that role,' he has said publicly.

But, even though Charles respected his wife's role as a mother, the underlying tensions between the pair surfaced almost from the moment William was born. Charles wanted to name him Arthur Albert. Diana was having none of it, and he was named William Arthur Philip Louis instead.

As the boys started to grow up they both displayed the type of good manners that their father insisted upon. Meeting people, they would offer a handshake and always made a point of writing thank-you notes. One of the more charming aspects of this for visitors to Kensington Palace or Highgrove was that the boys would come down in their dressing gowns to say goodnight. In fact, one of the few people not be immediately bowled over by the young princes was Sir Bob Geldof. He had come to Kensington Palace to discuss African famine with Charles when William sauntered in. Unsurprisingly, the dapper youngster was taken aback by the Irishman's appearance. He said, 'He's all dirty. He's got scruffy hair and wet shoes.' Never one to suffer fools, Sir Bob retorted, 'Shut up, you horrible little boy. Your hair's scruffy, too.'

'No it's not. My mother brushed it,' he chipped back.

Prince Charles believed the only way to ensure that his sons grew up with the type of traditional values he cherished was by employing an old-fashioned British nanny. He said: 'There are some experts who were very certain about how you should bring up children. But then, after twenty years, they turned round and said they'd been wrong. Think of all the poor people who had followed their suggestions.'

Diana was far more intent on following the teachings of an altogether more modern teacher in the shape of Dr Benjamin Spock, with whom she claimed a distant blood relationship. Spock was an influential advocate of the new permissive attitude towards childcare, and that was exactly what Diana wanted for her sons. As soon as William was born, Charles wanted to employ his old nanny, Mabel Anderson, who had played such a significant role in his life. Diana forcefully argued that Mabel was both too old and far too traditional for the job she had in mind. 'A mother's arms are so much more comforting than anyone else's,' she told him bluntly.

But she did accept that her position as the Princess of Wales meant she would need full-time support if she was to be able to carry out her public duties. Prince Charles soon realised that on this subject the lady was not for turning, so he finally agreed to Diana's choice of Barbara Barnes.

As if to draw a line under the past, she was the first royal nanny not to have at least two footmen and two housemaids to help her. 'I'm here to help the princess, not to take over,' Barbara tactfully announced. The daughter of a forestry worker, Barbara had an easy manner, which children responded to, and she got on well with the boys and even Prince Charles himself.

Ultimately, the relationship between Nanny Barnes and her employers began to unravel, mirroring the disintegration of feelings between Diana and her husband.

The princess began to see her as a rival for her sons' affections, and Charles was disturbed by the publication of pictures taken when Barbara had flown to the West Indies before Christmas 1986 for the sixtieth-birthday party of her former employer, Lord Glenconner, on his private island, Mustique.

She was photographed enjoying herself in the company of such fellow revellers as Princess Margaret, Jerry Hall and Raquel Welch. Charles did not approve, having old-fashioned views about staff knowing their places.

Inevitably, on 15 January 1987, it was announced that Barbara Barnes would be leaving. The statement was timed to coincide with William's first day at his new school. 'I thought no one would notice,' Diana later said, 'but I was wrong, wasn't I?' The British press did not miss a trick. Sensing a story, the tabloid editors elevated the news of Barbara's departure on the front page, and relegated William's arrival at his new pre-preparatory school to the inside pages.

Meanwhile, William was helping to set the stage for Harry to follow in his footsteps two years later. He quickly informed his new classmates, 'My daddy is a real prince.'

Another thing Diana was determined about was that neither of her beloved sons would go to Charles's old school Gordonstoun. One of her royal relations remarked, 'She's the strong one in the marriage, especially where it comes to the children.' Like many mothers at the time, the princess was adamant that her sons should be dressed in the most up-to-date fashion and was not going to be put off by stuffy royal protocol or so-called tradition. Out went the short trousers and velvet-collared coats of her husband's youth and in came striped T-shirts by Jean Bourget and sweatshirts and corduroy trousers from Benetton. She wanted them to be children of their generation, not throwbacks to the fifties.

Whereas the Queen and the Queen Mother had both left their children at home during their lengthy trips away, when Charles and Diana visited Woomargama in Australia, William was taken too, along with a supply of food supplements and fluoride drops. Sadly for the boys, it was over issues such as spending time with the kids that their parents were becoming ever more estranged. Michael Shea, the Queen's former press secretary, said, 'The only arguments they had were over the children.'

William and Harry reacted to these strains in their own way. William was always described as being forceful; his brother as sweet and a little reserved and shy. At Mrs Mynors's school Prince Harry had hidden in the playground and refused to join the other children in their games. But, as Harry grew older and his mischievous character came to the fore, it emerged that he was a better rider and more daring skier than his brother. 'Harry's the naughty one, just like me,' his mother said with a glint in her eye.

Harry also developed a passion for animals and the countryside. In fact, he started to echo his father's famous belief in talking to plants. 'Harry loves animals and plants,' Charles proudly observed. 'I tell him all about them and say they have feelings, too, and mustn't be hurt.'

William by contrast became more sensitive, introverted and closer to his mother. 'William is a very self-possessed, intelligent and mature boy and quite shy,' said his maternal uncle, Charles, now the ninth Earl Spencer. 'He is quite formal and stiff.'

Diana was always very close to her boys and would frequently hug them and kiss them. 'I want to bring them security. I hug my children to death and get into bed with them at night. I always feed them love and affection – it's so important.' This was an acutely difficult time for William and Harry, who were aware that there was severe tension between their parents.

William became concerned that he might be responsible for his mother's unhappiness. When she locked herself in the bathroom to cry uncontrollably, he tried to help by pushing tissues under the bathroom door.

After Nanny Barnes's sudden departure, Diana soon realised she would need help with the boys, and so she hired another nanny, Ruth Wallace, from her Kensington Palace neighbours, Prince and Princess Michael of Kent, and Jessie Webb, who had worked for the interior decorator Nina Campbell for fifteen years. The whole thing was presided over by the indomitable Olga Powell, who had started as under-nanny at the same time as Barbara Barnes. They were 'old-fashioned' nannies and subscribed to the Ps and Qs and the general politeness expected of any well-brought-up child. While Diana did not want her sons spoiled in any way, they still ended up showered with gifts. Barry Manilow gave Harry a valuable five-inch baby-grand piano and Jaguar presented William with a miniature motor car, which he crashed into the garage wall.

One year, William had a tea party in the insect house of London Zoo. In 1992, King Constantine of Greece gave him a cowboys-and-Indians party at his home in north London. Diana wore a cowgirl outfit and both William and Harry wore cowboy outfits. This was at the height of the speculation about the royal marriage, but Charles and Diana presented a united front in the presence of the children.

But by now their problems were too deep-rooted to be dismissed, and Prince Charles was staying away from the family home for days at a time.

When Sergeant Barry Mannakee, her former bodyguard – whom Diana had grown particularly fond of – was killed in a motor accident, Charles did not tell her straightaway. He waited until the car that was taking them to an official engagement came to a halt. Then, just as she was opening the door, he said, 'Mannakee's dead!' and pushed her out.

Their differences came to a public head when William was rushed to hospital in 1991 after being accidentally struck on the head by another boy's golf club at school. The school tried to keep the matter internal, and if it had not been for the quick thinking of William's protection officer, Sergeant Reg Spinney, the situation might have been much worse. He bleeped Diana's protection officer, Ken Wharfe, who broke the news of the accident to the princess during a lunch with friends at her favourite restaurant, San Lorenzo. After first being taken to the Royal Berkshire Hospital in Reading, William was transferred to the Great Ormond Street Hospital in London, where he was given a general anaesthetic and operated on for a depressed fracture of the skull.

Charles and Diana raced to the hospital, she from Knightsbridge and he from Highgrove. The princess was overcome with worry and insisted on staying at the hospital, but the prince said he had to attend a performance at Covent Garden with a party of European Community officials.

Diana was furious. Eventually, the couple realised they would have to separate and the boys were told by their parents. Their Christmas holiday that year would come to symbolise the difference in approach by Charles and Diana. They spent Christmas Day at Sandringham with their father, who had taken on his old nanny, Mabel Anderson. 'It's just like old times,' the Queen is said to have remarked.

When they rejoined Diana, it was very different. She whisked them off to the Caribbean for sea and sun, quite a contrast with bleak, flat Norfolk. For Diana, the difference was more than merely symbolic. She said that was determined that the boys would grow up in an emotionally healthier environment than she did herself.

Diana was only seven when her mother, then Viscountess Althorp, started proceedings in the High Court in London to end her fourteen-year marriage to the seventh Earl Spencer's son and heir, Johnnie. She was thirty-two, her husband was forty. The divorce was a bitter one that pitted husband against wife, turned Lady Althorp's mother, Ruth, Lady Fermoy, against her daughter, and eventually lost Lady Althorp the custody of her four children. It left Diana with emotional wounds from which she was still struggling to recover.

She told friends that she could vividly remember the arguments, the sounds of her mother crying and occasions when her father's temper drove him to violence.

For Diana, the scars would eventually resurface with the eating disorder, bulimia. 'Most bulimics have a history of early emotional starvation,' wrote the psychotherapist

Patricia Peters in a newspaper article. The concept is "My mother couldn't have loved me or she wouldn't have left me".'

The truth was that Frances fought in the courts to keep custody of Diana and her other children, Sarah, Jane and Charles. But the judge awarded Viscount Althorp custody, and ordered Diana's mother and her lover Peter Shand Kydd to pay the £3,000 legal costs. After the final split, Diana's brother, Charles, would cry himself to sleep at night, calling out for his mother. Sarah, Diana's older sister, would later develop anorexia nervosa, a disease closely related to bulimia.

For Diana, the damage of the traumatic divorce was compounded by the knowledge that her father wanted her to be a male child so he would have an heir. This situation came to be repeated later in life Charles wanting Harry to be a girl, and Diana would come to feel it. Diana herself was born on 1 July 1961. But, because Johnnie was so set upon having a son, he had chosen only boys' names, so it was a full week before she was named Diana Frances.

By that time Johnnie was blaming Frances for their failure to produce a son and she was ordered to Harley Street for tests. Diana later said poignantly, 'I was supposed to be a boy.'

In the summer of 1966 Frances met the wallpaper heir Peter Shand Kydd. They became lovers and Frances moved into a plush apartment in Cadogan Place in Chelsea to be near him. His pride hurt, Johnnie determined he would have care and control of all the children and get his wife back. Frances did return for the Christmas of 1967, but the couple rowed violently. Frances moved out and left Diana behind in the care of nannies.

Diana, Nanny Clarke said, was 'seriously affected' by the breakdown of her parents' marriage. Once so lively, the little girl the staff had nicknamed 'Duchess' became introverted and nervous and acquired the lifetime's habit of always looking down. But these experiences do help to explain why Diana was so fiercely determined that William and Harry should never be denied their mother's love.

As Diana herself noted, Harry had inherited her wicked sense of mischief. On one occasion at Mrs Mynors's the little prince was frogmarched to the headmistress by the distraught music teacher Mr Prichard. All through a morning assembly, Harry, who was sitting next to the piano, kept tugging at Mr Prichard's trousers as the teacher was trying to play. Eventually, the teacher had had enough.

'What on earth is it, Harry? Stop pulling my trousers,' he said.

'But Mr Prichard,' Harry piped up, 'I can see your willy.'

Harry's classmates thought this daring comment was hilarious and burst into fits of laughter. Mr Prichard, his face flushed red and his pride hurt, ejected the cheeky prince, who was sent straight to the headmistress for a dressing down.

It was not the first time he had overstepped the mark, and the head decided to discuss the issue with the princess. But Ken Wharfe, Diana's personal protection officer at the time, recalled that she did not get the kind of reaction she was perhaps hoping for. For when the teacher spelled out her concerns the princess could not contain herself and burst into a fit of giggles.

Ken Wharfe later recalled, 'By the time I was assigned to head up the protection for William and Harry in 1986 it was already clear to the inner circle of royal courtiers and friends of both the prince and princess that, after just five years, their marriage was in serious difficulties. But both parents dearly loved their boys and at first did their best to shield them both from the worst excesses of their disintegrating relationship.

'The role of wife and mother was the one Diana valued most highly. She would go to great lengths to protect that. I witnessed her commitment and concerns for her two young sons. Charles loved his sons desperately but, sadly by this time, not his wife. For this reason, from early on, Diana focused all her love on her boys,' he said.

Many holidays with William and Harry were spent without their father. Security was essential and the affable Scotland Yard officers accompanied Diana and her sons on most, if not all, of these private holidays. The locations visited were indeed the resorts of the privileged – the Island of Nevis, the Bahamas, Necker Island (owned by Sir Richard Branson) – but, irrespective of location, Diana was determined that her sons would have fun. And they did. With the resources of a loving energetic mother, how could they fail to? Irrespective of her royal commitments, William and Harry were Diana's priority, and they knew it.

'With the exception of unavoidable official public duties, I do not recall Diana missing one "school run",' Wharfe recalled. 'The opportunity to talk through their school day with "Mummy" on the short car journey from Kensington Palace to both kindergarten at Jane Mynors's and pre-prep at the Wetherby School was an invaluable time for the boys and one I felt very privileged to be part of. Once at school, Diana would take her place in any queue of waiting parents to chat informally with respective head teachers of school, something Diana relished. Both William and Harry loved this aspect of their mother's involvement.'

Whatever their personal difficulties, Charles and Diana always put their differences aside when it came to their sons. Happiness and the 'normal' ingredient were always evident, whether it was organising the 'Nevis Toad Derby' – a race the boys devised to make money from bets on the island's giant toads – or bombarding the press boats with water balloons for breaking the agreement not to take pictures, a fight the future soldier-princes relished. (More on these incidents later.) Diana was always in on their *Just William* pranks, and her authority to proceed was always sought and never denied.

If anything, Diana encouraged Harry's mischievous nature. It manifested itself one morning while they were on the school run. In the car leaving Kensington Palace to go to Wetherby School were the chauffeur, the police protection officer, the princess and William and Harry. At that time, Diana loved nothing better telling risqué jokes to her entourage and was apparently unconcerned that her children were all ears.

On this particular day the protection officer did his best to dissuade her from telling her latest joke but in typical fashion she was having none of it. In fact, in true Diana style, the more he tried to stop her, the more determined she was to get the gag in.

Unfortunately for Diana two things were to collide that morning. She had an appointment with the headmistress, Frederika Blair-Turner, of whom Diana was terrified and was noticeably hyper at the prospect of the meeting; and, unfortunately for Diana, Harry was all ears as he listened to the joke, which he was determined to tell everybody when he arrived at school.

On Diana's arrival at Wetherby, Miss Blair-Turner was

waiting in the hallway, adjacent to the stairwell, and Diana, for reasons known only to her, decided she would have her meeting there and then. William ran off to his classroom but by now Harry was all fired up with the new joke he had just learned and began trying to tell it to his headmistress.

A horrified Diana went as red as a lobster as she realised what he was trying to do and tried very hard to stop him from telling it. At that point a sweating princess made a desperate appeal to her protection officer for help, but he declined, much to her chagrin, as she made plain later.

Fortunately, with so many interruptions and Harry's tenuous grasp of English, he was unable to get the joke out. Afterwards, Diana admitted to her protection officer that she thought she was on the verge of vomiting while Harry was holding court. The joke, as told to William and Harry:

'Why can't a Frenchwoman count up to seventy?' Because when she gets to sixty-nine she has a frog in her throat.' Miss Blair-Turner was horrified when told later that day just what had caused the commotion.

To say that royal children are brought up differently is something of an understatement. During my research for this book I discovered many fascinating insights into the young Prince Harry. One of my favourite stories I heard about the boys concerns a visit to Wookey Hole in Somerset. William and Harry, together with a couple of other children, visited the spot when Harry was about two years old. It was quite a long walk, and Harry was carried around by the adults in the party, being passed to each in turn, among them the nanny; but, to the puzzlement of all present, Harry would periodically burst into tears. Each time, the party came to a halt but the sobbing child was unable to explain what was wrong; and, when he stopped crying, the group set off again until the crying began once more.

It wasn't until the fourth outburst that the reason emerged. As Harry was passed from one adult to the next, he was 'bumped up'. Given that the cave has very low ceilings and he kept hitting his head, Harry ended the day not very happy, several bumps forming on his head, but fortunately for all concerned not able to tell his mother what had happened.

Harry was about six or seven years old when he displayed behaviour that demonstrated that he had inherited his mother's wilful streak. He was at Highgrove House, being entertained by one of his protection officers, who was giving him driving lessons in his father's Range Rover Discovery. The Scotland Yard officer was in the driving seat, Harry standing in the footwell, having access to the steering wheel, the front edge of the driver's seat and the accelerator.

After a while, Harry was informed that it was game over and time to take the car back, but he was having none of it and, as one of his protection team observed, he could be like a little Rottweiler when he didn't want to stop doing something.

Despite vigorous protests from the young prince, the protection officer insisted the car had to be taken back to where it was 'borrowed' from. Harry, still protesting, was now approaching the parking point, which just happened to be face-on to a rather large Cotswold stone wall. As he got closer Harry stamped hard down on the accelerator and pushed his bottom back, and the vehicle smacked into the wall. No damage was ever found on the vehicle!

Another of William and Harry's police protection officers often used the phrase 'I'm going to see a man about a dog' when he wished to go and do something that he wished neither of them to be privy to. The officer, who inherited the phrase from his family, used it constantly for the same purpose.

On one occasion at Highgrove, with both William and Harry present, the officer, having mentioned to both that he would be away for some time, was badgered incessantly by Harry as to the real reason he was going to be absent. This badgering was so constant and insistent that even William couldn't stand it any more – and he wanted to know, too. So, to shut Harry up, William said to him, 'Harry shut up, he's already told you: he's going dog-watching. Now shut up!'

Highgrove House was the setting for another encounter of the close kind. The hayloft was full to the brim, it being that time of the year. This was a favourite play area for the children and the protection officers loved it because the risk of injury was fairly low. Harry had clambered up to the higher reaches and then announced he had to pee. (By now, the protection team had learned that, when either Harry or William announced he needed a pee, then he would go, no matter where he was.)

Harry started to pee out of the open side of the hayloft, which induced in the protection officer a desperate need to relieve himself. But, just as the officer joined in, he heard Prince Charles calling for his sons. Somehow he managed to stop, but Harry couldn't. Charles approached from ground level and, staying out of range, established he had found Harry and asked if William was there as well, because he had spotted two streams of pee when he rounded the corner. 'Oh that's just the policeman Papa, but he's stopped now.'

'Oh, wonderful!' was the reply.

Despite his naughtiness, Harry demonstrated he was a tough little chap from an early age. When he was big enough he inherited from William a Shetland pony, which was kept at Highgrove. From the moment Harry first rode it, the pony seemed to take on its new owner's personality and started doing exactly as it pleased. It refused to be led or ridden as the mood took it, and it seized every opportunity to bolt off with Harry in the saddle, run for anything from a quarter to half a mile, find the nearest stream and dump Harry in it.

The scene was straight out of a Thelwell book, with the minimum of a groom and protection officer, both on foot, trying to catch up with, let alone catch, the beast, with William also in hand, and finding Harry in all sorts of bushes, streams and hedgerows. It was a running joke among the staff that, if Harry had been living in a normal home, he would have been taken into care because of his injuries.

Harry's biggest problem was always that he just couldn't get the message when he was really playing up and was being told to calm down. On one particularly long car journey, William and Harry had started to play up and were really getting up the noses of the chauffeur, the nanny and protection officer. Despite repeated warnings from the nanny, the boys continued to misbehave and it was clear that trouble was imminent.

As usual it was William who was the main offender and William who finally got the message. Not Harry. Driven to distraction, the protection officer ordered the car to stop. It did – but so suddenly that the backup car nearly crashed into its rear. By now, the officer had dragged Harry out of the car, taken him around to the back of the car and, standing in the road, foot on the rear bumper of the royal car, put Harry across his knee, pulled down his trousers and smacked him. Blissful silence ensued for at least a half mile.

The only person who was ever able to get the better of Harry on a consistent basis was his nanny, Jessie. A large woman, she discovered the simple but effective technique of pinning Harry to the wall of his nursery with her stomach. On many occasions, his delighted protection officers were treated to the sight of a squirming Harry suspended off the floor, against a wall and somewhere inside the ample girth of Nanny Jessie.

The soldier-prince had a good grounding from the royal staff, and he soon learned that, despite his royal rank, there was a pecking order. It would stand him in good stead for his future career.

CHAPTER FOUR

BOY SOLDIER

'Harry is really into soldiers at the moment.'
PRINCESS DIANA TO ARMY WIVES ABOUT HER
THEN EIGHT-YEAR-OLD SON

Hindsight, they say, is always 20/20 and, as one looks back through Harry's eventful life, it isn't difficult to pinpoint the first public moment when it became obvious that he was determined to follow a military career. It was 29 July 1993, his parents' twelfth wedding anniversary, and Harry accompanied his mother on an official visit to the Light Dragoons Regiment at Bergen-Hohne Barracks, Germany. To add to the excitement, his big brother William had been left at home. To some eight-year-old boys it would have been a daunting debut. A battery of newspapermen and photographers, myself among them, then as royal correspondent of the *Daily Express*, waited for young Harry.

When he first arrived, he appeared a little shy and we all wondered if he would end up hiding behind the princess throughout the visit. We needn't have worried. Diana, as usual, was resplendent, this time in a sky-blue suit that complemented her tall and slender frame perfectly. Harry was turned out in a smart blazer and grey trousers and looked every inch the little English gentleman. As he stayed close to his mother and gripped his hands tightly together behind his back, the pair inspected the immaculately turned-out soldiers of the Light Dragoons, who were decked out in their formal black uniforms topped off with red caps.

At one point Diana placed a reassuring arm around her son's shoulder to let him know how well he was coping with an assignment that she feared might leave him overawed. But, with the first part of the engagement completed, Harry was itching for the next. It was clear that his initial nerves had dissolved amid the excitement of what was to follow. While Diana spoke to troops at the base near Hanover, Harry was being kitted out in his own army uniform made especially for him after the regiment's quartermaster had phoned the palace for his measurements. When he reappeared in public the young prince had been transformed into a little action man and was wearing camouflage fatigues topped off with a beret.

Then, with a touch of camouflage paint applied to his face, he was taken to a Scimitar tank and now the slightly nervous expression had been replaced by a beaming smile that split his face from ear to ear. As the vehicle rumbled off, he was clearly in his element as he 'directed operations' from the tank turret, then slipped back inside when it was ambushed in a mock attack.

Machine guns rattled out blank rounds as the tank emerged through the multicoloured smoke. He was so engrossed that he committed the soldier's gravest error: jumping down to greet his mother, he forgot his briefing to salute her, and waved instead. She laughed, as did the officers accompanying her.

The princess revealed the reason for Prince William's absence while chatting to wives of a hundred soldiers serving in the United Nations peacekeeping force in Bosnia. Louise Laverick, then twenty-eight, said, 'I asked her why he wasn't here. She said, "I would have brought them both but they'd have fought over the tank, so I left William at home. Harry is really into soldiers at the moment."'

It was to prove more than a fleeting moment, too. On that summer's day the little boy had made up his mind: he was going to be a soldier and he wouldn't let anyone or anything stand in his way. Almost thirteen years later, almost to the day, Harry was back in an armoured army vehicle again, but this time for real. At twenty-one, the prince presented a very different picture at the helm as he fulfilled his childhood dream of a military life. He was photographed wearing his communications helmet and protective goggles as he drove an armoured reconnaissance vehicle after having successfully completed the signals phase of his troop leaders' course at Bovington in Dorset.

It came as no surprise to Ken Wharfe, Diana's personal protection officer, who had developed a close bond with Harry during his formative years after arriving on the royal scene to head up security for the two young princes in November 1987. Harry, he recalled, was always a handful, a mischievous boy who was full of fun. 'He had a twinkle in his eye, and you never knew quite what to expect with Harry,' the former Scotland Yard inspector said.

When he took the job, Diana joked, 'I don't fancy your job, Ken.' He had been summoned to Sandringham, Norfolk, to meet the princess and his new charges for the first time, and Harry, as ever, made quite a first impression. Wharfe recalled, 'I was shown into one of the many rooms, to watch William attempting to play the piano as Harry was trying to pull the stamens from the arrangement of lilies on a nearby table.'

As the princess caught him giving Harry a quizzical look, she joked, 'They're a liability' as she cast an eye over her beloved sons. William overheard her and swivelled round on his piano stool. 'No we're not, we are reliability,' he chipped in. Diana started to laugh, and so did William, at which point the vase of lilies toppled from the table and crashed to the floor. Harry decided to make a sharp exit followed by his brother and their mother in hot pursuit. Ken met up with the princess a little later and she asked, 'I suppose that was normal this morning?' Ken replied, 'What, ma'am? The piano or the lilies?' and the two roared with laughter.

It was the beginning of an excellent working relationship between the princess and the policeman that would last for another seven years. Wharfe developed an avuncular bond with Harry and William, which the princess encouraged. And, although nobody could take the place in their affections of their beloved 'Papa', it is fair to say that Ken was a positive male influence over the young princes as the relationship between their parents deteriorated. The boys always knew he was there primarily to keep them safe from harm, but he was fun, too, and they enjoyed his being close by when he accompanied them around the world on private holidays, often without their father.

Harry was just three when Ken first started working in royalty protection. The officer recalled that the young prince was always a boisterous child and always mad about the army and soldiers. It was like an obsession. The inspector recalled, 'Every birthday or Christmas, whenever Harry was asked what he wanted for his main present, his response was always the same: "An army uniform – I really need a camouflage jacket."' Invariably, his mother caved in to his persistence.

On weekdays he would accompany the princess when she took William to Wetherby prep school in Notting Hill, a short distance from Kensington Palace, their London home, where several other members of the Royal Family had grace-and-favour apartments. The same routine was put in place for Harry, too, when he was old enough. The weekends would be spent at Highgrove, the Gloucestershire estate Charles bought in August 1980, not quite a year before his marriage, for around £750,000. Set in 348 well-wooded acres on the edge of the picturesque Cotswolds, about two hours' drive west of London, it was where Charles in particular felt at home and able to forget the pressures of public life; the princess and her sons, too – despite claims to the contrary – grew to like the place.

Diana's love for her sons was absolute and consistent. Charles, too, when he was around, was an attentive father, but his hectic work schedule meant that the royal princes spent more time with their mother and the policeman than him. The royal brothers would often engage in play fights with the police officer, attacking him in the police room he occupied in Kensington Palace. On occasion they were making so much noise that Charles came in to check he was all right. 'They can be a little rough,' Charles said.

Harry always fought to win and he didn't mind fighting dirty, either. On many occasions, as Ken tried to fend off his attack, the prince would aim a fierce punch into his private parts, knowing it was where it would hurt most.

Harry was enthralled with the business of security. He was always plaguing his police bodyguards to use their radios and to show them the guns they carried. 'He was a pain in the backside,' Wharfe explained. One day the experienced Scotland Yard officer relented and it could have had serious repercussions. Luckily, not least for the inspector, it all ended happily. Harry arrived unannounced in his room and asked if he could use the radio. At first Ken refused, but the prince would not take no for an answer.

'Please, Ken, can I use the radio? I just want to see how it works,' he pleaded. After several minutes Wharfe relented and, after he had given Harry specific instructions on how to use it, the two of them worked out a plan. Harry was to go to set points within the Kensington Palace compound, which was guarded twenty-four hours a day by static protection, and check in. It seemed harmless enough but Ken, for once, had failed to take into consideration the Harry factor. The young prince was ecstatic: it was his chance to act like a real police officer and he promised not to let Ken down.

For the next few minutes Ken received regular check calls and Harry followed the inspector's instructions to the letter. The two had agreed that he could visit his aunt, Lady Jane Fellowes, in the stable block, just a short distance from the entrance of Kensington Palace, but still within CCTV coverage. Ken made a quick check call to Lady Jane, who confirmed Harry had arrived safely. A short while later, Lady Jane telephoned him to say that Harry had just left and was on his way back towards the police barrier. But Harry did not show. 'I was getting a bit anxious, so I telephoned the police box, but the duty officer told me he hadn't seen Harry.'

Faced with a potential security disaster of his own making that would have graced any newspaper front page, Ken was about to send out a search party when in the nick of time Harry radioed in.

'Harry, can you hear me?' Ken said hopefully and as calmly as possible. 'Where the hell are you?'

'Ken, Harry calling, over,' he said. 'I am at Tower Records in High Street, Kensington,' he continued without a care in the world. Ken could see his exemplary career crashing about him. He was lucky that the radio had the ability to transmit over the extra distance.

'What on earth are you doing there, Harry?' he barked. 'Report back to me as soon as possible,' he said. Within minutes the boy was back safely. 'I gave him a serious ticking off for disobeying specific orders,' Ken said. The officer knew it had ultimately been his responsibility and he certainly would have been blamed if something had happened. It was an important lesson for the pair of them. Undoubtedly, his Scotland Yard bosses would have taken a very dim view of it, but it would have been as nothing compared with Diana's wrath. Fortunately, neither of them found out. Harry knew he had breached the deal and he kept quiet too.

Even before the split, many of the family holidays were spent without Charles. Security was essential, so the bodyguard would accompany the princess and her sons to exotic locations, where she could recharge her batteries from the excesses of public life. Her priority was always her sons. Unless it was impossible, she never missed a school run. She encouraged her boys to be boys, to enjoy themselves just like other youngsters of their age.

Diana was always in on their *Just William*-style pranks,

most of which could have come straight from the pages of Richmal Compton's books about the naughty schoolboy, William. But they certainly weren't of just William's making: Harry was the instigator of many of them. Her authority to proceed was always sought and never denied them.

During one weekend at Highgrove, Diana had arranged a surprise go-karting event for her sons. It was not at a preordained circuit, but within the grounds of Highgrove. Early on a Saturday morning, Martin Howell, owner of Playscape Racing in South London, arrived with four karts. Harry was ecstatic and he and William rushed off to plan the circuit. Within minutes, after the Dutch barn had been turned into the pits, the Highgrove Formula One circuit was about to be raced. Unbeknown to the princess, the last hairpin happened to run through Charles's kitchen garden, with a final straight running through the recently seeded wildflower meadow.

With the practice laps over, the race began and ended with William and Harry both taking positions on four erected straw bales. There was no champagne but a bottle of their papa's prized lemon refresher was enjoyed by all. The only casualties were the prince's free-roaming chickens that took fight as the karts approached the finishing line, resulting in their keepers, local police officers assigned to the house, having to explain to His Royal Highness why there was a drop in egg-laying.

A week later, again at Highgrove, Charles had a quiet word with Inspector Wharfe, who had facilitated Diana's plan, and who had learned of the adventure from an excited Harry. 'Thankfully he did not mention the chickens, but he did remark on the muddied tracks through the wildflower beds.'

Poor Ken thought Diana would have told her husband beforehand. 'I told him that both William and Harry had had a fun-packed day and, desperate to escape any further questioning, I excused myself before the prince, with another dropped grin, said, "Oh, really? Do you fancy being the next Bernie Eccleston?"'

But by the early 1990s, no matter how hard the royal couple tried to put a brave face on their failing relationship in public, in private they both knew it was over. Both had been indulging in extramarital affairs, Charles with the married Camilla Parker Bowles and Diana with a number of suitors, but most notably with the dashing cavalry officer James Hewitt. Those close to the family knew it was only a matter of time before the marriage would implode; what they did not know was how it would impact upon the couple's two young sons.

The Queen called 1992 her '*annus horribilis*'. She was not wrong. Without doubt it was one of the most difficult years for the Royal Family since the abdication crisis of 1936. The publication of Andrew Morton's biography *Diana: Her True Story*, with which Diana cooperated, was the beginning of the end. It labelled Charles a cheating, abusive husband and suggested he was not up to the top job as King. Worse, as far as the palace were concerned, was the fact that Diana's friends and family were quoted at length throughout it. Senior members of the Royal Family, as well as powerful courtiers, were convinced of the princess's involvement, despite her denials.

Then there was the announcement of the separation of the Duke and Duchess of York, Princess Anne's divorce from Captain Mark Phillips and the fire at Windsor Castle.

The Queen could have been forgiven for thinking fate was conspiring against her.

It was a particularly difficult year for Charles and Diana's sons, too. Their grandfather, Earl Spencer, died while they were on a skiing holiday in Lech, Austria, which only demonstrated the emotional chasm between their warring parents. Harry was just eight when his parents' separation was announced in the House of Commons by the incumbent Conservative Prime Minister John Major in December 1992. Unlike his brother William, who acted as Diana's emotional crutch throughout her tormented marriage with Charles, Harry was largely shielded from his mother's fluctuating emotions. He also adored his papa; they had a close bond and Charles always adored Harry's rebellious, risqué streak.

Diana always saw William as her champion and he had a natural knack of supporting the princess when she needed it most. He assumed the role of supportive son and had reached that rewarding age when the child becomes a companion and a friend to his parent, able to appreciate, at least in part, a parent's troubles. Whenever Diana felt uncertain, William was there. He once told her he wanted to be a policeman so that he could protect her. Her heart must have ached with his earnest sincerity. When the divorce was finalised and it emerged that the princess would be stripped of her royal title, it was William who threw his arms around her and exclaimed, 'Don't worry, Mummy, I'll give it back to you one day, when I'm King.' It made her cry even more.

Sometimes she went too far, burdening William with problems and paranoia he should never have been asked to shoulder. Patrick Jephson, Diana's well-respected private secretary, confided that the princess herself admitted being afraid that William, like her, was too sensitive for the part he must play in the Royal Family. Yet she continued to load his young mind with her troubles regardless, while every embarrassing indiscretion was played out in the press.

Those who served the princess at the time say that she had no such qualms about Harry. She always felt he was robust enough to deal with anything. 'William doesn't want to be King, and I worry about that,' she told her butler, Paul Burrell. 'He doesn't want his every move watched.' She went on to telephone her American friend Lana Marks to express the same worries. The princess empathised with her son who, like his mother, was naturally shy and retiring.

Paul Burrell said Diana always thought Harry was a better prospect and, having observed the two boys at close quarters, he agreed. Burrell went on, 'He [William] had been born second in line to the throne. At the time, Harry's attributes and attitude almost made him more of a realistic prospect to take on the onerous duties of the monarch. He was more outgoing and pragmatic.

'Harry would see no problem in taking on the job,' the princess told Burrell. 'GKH. That's what we'll call him. GKH for Good King Harry. I like that!' From then on, whenever Harry was with Diana for the weekend, the princess used the secret code to refer to him. It was an affectionate nickname, one she shared with two other close friends as well as Burrell, even if Harry never knew. He would need the courage of the past English kings who shared his name to cope with the next traumatic episode of his young life.

The princess did everything she could to shield her sons.

In January 1993, within weeks of the announcement of the divorce, and after they had spent a traditional Christmas at Sandringham, the princess whisked them off to Nevis, the tiny island in the northern Leeward chain in the eastern Caribbean. All hell was breaking out at home and the strain was beginning to tell on Diana. She could not stand another day and needed to escape the media frenzy with her sons. It would be difficult to imagine a more idyllic setting. The Montpelier Plantation Inn, owned by the charming English couple James and Celia Milnes-Gaskill, was set in 16 acres surrounded by secluded gardens and stone terraces, with sixteen exclusive luxury chalets dotted around the grounds. Privacy was the watchword and it was to prove the perfect hideaway.

The princess and her sons soon settled into their holiday routine. Diana, armed with a few well-thumbed Jackie Collins novels and with her friend Catherine Soames as a companion, was able to relax in the sun, splashing in the surf with her boys, wearing her bright-orange bikini. She was determined to look good when the press eventually caught up, and a golden tan was essential. The first day was media-free, and, while their mother loved to relax, sunbathing on her lounger, William and Harry were always restless and seeking out new adventures on holiday.

Harry was invariably the instigator. He decided to kidnap some of the island's indigenous population, although, thankfully, it did not involve abducting a local tribe, just a dozen giant toads. He had spotted the creatures, which were about 9 inches long, in the undergrowth, and set about capturing them. A big hunt was on. The princes, the hotel owners' children and the police bodyguards joined in, although Diana refused to partake in the safari; she did, however, remain in the background, shrieking with laughter as they tried to ensnare the unfortunate creatures. 'What on earth are you going to do with them now you've caught them, boys?' she asked, dreading the answer. 'You'll see, Mummy – just wait and see,' Harry replied.

The entire party was then instructed to rendezvous on the lush green lawn at the back of the Montpelier, where Harry revealed his master plan: in essence, a chance for the boys to make some money. After the healthiest-looking creatures had been selected, everyone was then invited to pick a runner for what Harry called the 'Nevis Toad Derby', a race over 15 feet for which the prince was taking bets. Harry's grand plan backfired, as most of the toads just legged it back into the undergrowth as quick as they could, hoping never to encounter a British royal again. Everyone just fell about laughing. It was a typical Harry prank, and was not the first.

On a holiday to Necker Island a year earlier, when the press did eventually track down the royal party, Harry and William came up with a plan to punish them for intruding on their privacy. Sir Richard Branson's manager on the island had returned from one of his business trips to Tortola armed with three giant catapults and hundreds of balloons, which he gave to the children, including their cousin 'Beatle', the son of Diana's sister, Lady Jane, and brother-in-law, Sir Robert Fellowes, the Queen's private secretary. The warrior in Harry loved his new weapons. Once they had tired of firing water-filled balloons at each other, the royal princes had a brainwave. William sought his bodyguard's approval. 'Ken,' he said, his eyes lighting up, 'when the photographers come back in their boats, why don't we catapult them from the house?' There was a perfect vantage point, set upon rocks about 80 feet from the shoreline. The royal brothers – whose ancestors had led troops into battle – and their cousin set about constructing two sites in readiness for the arrival of the press flotilla.

When Diana found out about her sons' battle plans she thought it was hilarious and sanctioned their entire military operation. With the bodyguards supervising, the boys prepared for battle and, true to form, the boats carrying the hardcore paparazzi approached. His face beaming, Harry unleashed the first of the stack of water balloons. The unsuspecting photographers didn't know what had hit them, and after a twenty-minute assault retired hurt and did not return (perhaps seeing the funny side). Harry and William rushed back to their mother, bursting with pride at their achievement. Harry, the soldier-prince, had notched up his first victory in battle; it would not be his last.

CHAPTER FIVE

GOODBYE, MUMMY

Prince Charles may have been rather stuffy as far as his public image was concerned, but he undoubtedly did his best to be a good father to his sons. He loved both William and Harry dearly. He did not want them to fear him, as he did his own father, and perhaps, as a result, was soft with them. He was never a disciplinarian; it was just not his style.

After the separation the boys' time was divided equally between their parents. The experience could not have been more diverse. With the princess they enjoyed the 'normality' she wanted for them: trips to Thorpe Park, Walt Disney World, McDonald's. With their father they enjoyed the 'manly' pursuits that their mother so violently disapproved of. But, no matter how much she tried to turn their heads with thrilling adventures, they made it clear they were devoted to their father too.

Harry loved the Windsor way. As a boy he learned to

shoot on the royal estates of Sandringham and Balmoral, and revelled in the lifestyle. Diana knew there was no way she could stop him, and, perhaps operating under the theory of 'if you can't beat them, join them', she even asked her bodyguards to arrange a visit to Lippetts Hill, the Metropolitan Police firearms training unit, to try out the weapons. Harry was in his element as he fired live rounds into the targets.

When the boys were with their father they spent a great deal of time with their cousins, Princess Anne's children Peter and Zara Phillips, who themselves had lived through the pain of the very public breakdown of their parents' marriage. Charles, perhaps stung by adverse reports, worried that when they were with him he was not providing them with enough homeliness. He felt something was lacking, but his solution was to infuriate Diana in a way that he, due to his upbringing, probably could never have imagined. He hired a nanny, thirty-year-old Tiggy Legge-Bourke, to act as a quasi-surrogate mother, and to inject some zest into his boys' life when they stayed with him.

She enjoyed hunting, shooting and fishing and acted more like a big sister than a conventional royal nanny. She became somebody both boys could confide in without fear of reprisals. It is fair to say they loved her to bits. However, racked by guilt and a lack of self-belief, Diana saw Tiggy as a threat. She was unimpressed with Charles's plan and let him know it, convinced that it was part of a plot to turn her sons against her. Charles's response was to change nothing, but he asked Tiggy to keep a lower profile when she was out with the boys in public.

It did not quite work out that way. Harry's love of guns attracted adverse publicity too. On 20 April 1997, just a few months before Diana's death, Tiggy was at the centre of another row. Harry was photographed shooting rabbits hanging out of the widow from the back seat of a Land Rover at the age of twelve. The princess was furious, probably more due to the antipathy she felt towards Miss Legge-Bourke, who she feared was stepping into her maternal role, than to the fact that her son was behaving irresponsibly.

Diana may have had a point about her son's overfamiliar relationship with Tiggy. On one occasion Harry was caught putting his hand down Tiggy's front, near her breasts, as a joke when they travelled on a plane. She just laughed it off, saying, 'Boys will be boys, I suppose; he's got to learn.' But his protection officer did not see it that way and gave the prince a severe ticking off for his impudent behaviour.

Diana's paranoia boiled over in June 1997, when she decided to stay away from the traditional parents' picnic day at Eton College. She had not wanted to steal the spotlight and spoil everyone's fun. She made the sacrifice willingly, but when she learned that William had asked for Tiggy in her place, and that she had brought bottles of champagne and offered them to people Diana knew, she went ballistic. She was there at the invitation of William and Harry and they were having fun with her; but Diana didn't see it that way. 'That bitch!' she exclaimed when she heard. Of course, it was an overreaction born out of jealousy.

In July 1997, a month after her outburst over Tiggy, the princess and her sons enjoyed what turned out to be their last holiday together. They spent it in the South of France. Diana was nursing a broken heart after deciding to end her relationship with the Pakistani heart surgeon Hasnat Khan, a man she had hoped to marry. Perhaps in an attempt to make him feel jealous, the princess accepted a longstanding offer of an all-expenses-paid holiday, courtesy of Mohamed al-Fayed. Despite his controversial reputation, al-Fayed had been a friend of the princess's family for many years and she thought it would be good for William and Harry to mix with his young children, Karim, Jasmine, Camilla and Omar.

She was right: the boys' had a ball at the Villa Castel Ste-Thérèse, set high on the cliffs above St-Tropez, in a 10-acre estate complete with its own private beach and the luxurious private yacht, the *Jonikal*, at their constant disposal. Harry loved it and, apart from a spat with one of al-Fayed's sons (in which he emerged the victor), he had a ball. The boys spent their days jet skiing, scuba diving or simply lounging around the pool.

Never one to miss a trick, al-Fayed demanded his eldest son Dodi join them, which he did without telling his girlfriend, the model Kelly Fisher. It was then that the romance began between the princess and the playboy. The two had met at a polo match in July 1986, but this time, in the relaxed environment of the Côte d'Azur, something clicked between them. One evening at supper it spilled over, as some light-hearted teasing ended in a full-blown food fight, leaving everyone in hysterics.

On 20 July Diana and her boys flew back to London in al-Fayed's private Harrods jet. That evening she hugged and kissed them both before they went on to Balmoral to be reunited with their father for the summer. None of them knew it then, but it was to be the last time Harry and William would see their mother. With her sons packed off to Charles, Diana faced the prospect of a lonely summer. So, when the attentive Dodi, who had lavished gifts on her, then offered to whisk her away, she saw no reason to rebuff him. They enjoyed a romantic cruise to Corsica and Sardinia on 31 July. They were the only VIPs aboard the yacht; this was a love cruise.

The exact nature of the relationship has been much debated – not least in the inquest into the princess's death a decade later. Some say it was a holiday romance; others, such as Dodi's father, maintain that it was much more serious and that they would have married and she was expecting his child. Unbeknown to the princess, he spent the night with his American model while seducing Princess Diana by day, so the motivation behind Dodi's actions is unclear.

Perhaps, as Diana's close friend Rosa Monckton insisted, it was only ever a holiday romance, and by the end of the summer Diana had grown tired of his attentions. But, due to the extraordinary and tragic events that were to unfold over the next few weeks, their names would be entwined in history for ever.

Diana called William from the Imperial Suite of the Fayed-owned Ritz Hotel in Paris on 30 August 1997. Both boys could not wait to see her after a month apart.

William and Harry were both asleep when the first reports came through that something was wrong. At around 1 a.m., the Prince of Wales was awoken and told by telephone that his ex-wife had been injured in a car crash in the Pont de l'Alma tunnel in Paris. Dodi, he was told, was dead, Diana seriously injured. Charles, stunned by what he had heard, woke the Queen and Prince Philip. Then, moments later, came the awful news that the mother of his boys was dead. Racked with emotion, the unfortunate man broke down and wept.

The Queen, a cool head in a crisis, advised against waking the princes. She wisely counselled that they would need all the strength they could muster in the days that would follow. It was best to let them sleep while they still could. When the moment came, he would have to break the terrible news to his boys that they would never see their beloved mother again. He paced the corridors of Balmoral, overcome by the enormity of the task. He went alone to the moors, mulling over what he would say.

Then, at 7 a.m., he returned. William was already awake. Charles, his eyes ringed red and swollen by tears and lack of sleep, went into his elder son's room to break the news. The thoughts of both father and son turned to Harry, who was still asleep in the room next door. They decided to break the news together, explaining as gently as they could that the princess had been injured and the medical team had done everything in their power to save her. Now embracing each other, they wept uncontrollably as a unit, the sounds of their raw pain echoing around the old house. Nothing would be the same again for any of them.

The outward courage both princes displayed was amazing and showed a great inner strength. In the sombre moments that followed his mother's death, William, who had lost so much, proved a tower of strength to his younger brother. Those in her inner circle were amazed at how well he coped in the immediate aftermath of her death. Harry was more of a worry. The impish little boy all but disappeared; he retreated into himself.

On the day of the funeral, 6 September 1997, however, he showed the raw courage of a soldier. When Prince Charles suggested that he would walk behind their late mother's cortège, Harry was the first to say he would join him. William flatly refused. It was not until Prince Philip and Earl Spencer were also included that William went along with the idea. The tension was electric as the princes, heads bowed, passed Buckingham Palace. Outside, the Queen, who had been publicly criticised for her cool response since the death of the princess, led other members of the Royal Family in bowing as the cortège passed. Above them, from the flagstaff on the palace roof, the Union Flag fluttered at half-mast. It was the first time in history that it had been flown thus for anyone other than a monarch. That day, Diana's boys became men. Nothing would ever faze them again.

As a single parent, Prince Charles did his best to fill the emotional gap left by Diana's tragic death. But Charles, for all his qualities, could not be both mother and father. He did his best to steer his sons by what he describes as 'communicating an atmosphere of greater relaxation', or, in other words, using kindness and reason rather than binding his sons by a set of strict rules. This particularly applied to Harry, who always seemed so easygoing, confident and self-assured that he could deal with anything.

Charles disliked confrontations of any kind. There were times, however, when the wisdom of this approach was questioned, even by the Queen, when friends of his observed how unruly his two sons had become. On one occasion at Balmoral, for instance, they arrived late for lunch at one of the shooting lodges. Charles asked them sit at the table with his guests but they totally ignored his request, causing him huge embarrassment, saying they wanted to eat with the ghillies (hunt attendants or gamekeepers) outside. As they disappeared, Charles raised his hands in exasperation and said, 'What can I do?'

Perhaps, to those gathered there, the answer was to take a firmer hand. But Charles preferred to let them get away with it.

Diana might have acted differently; but Charles – particularly in the immediate aftermath of her death – didn't have the will or inclination for a more disciplinary approach. She expected good manners from her sons, something she prided herself on despite her own erratic behaviour. She often warned them never to be rude to staff. But, while William followed her rules to the letter, Harry showed some of the more volatile tendencies of his paternal grandfather, the Duke of Edinburgh.

Diana would often say Harry was the naughty one. He had a self-confidence that bordered on arrogance. He was always willing to have a go at anything, whereas his older brother was more cautious. Staff complained that, when they asked Harry when he wanted his lunch, he would say dismissively, 'I'll let you know later,' whereas William would always be specific.

In fact, the only person who could say anything to him was Tiggy Legge-Bourke, his 'nanny' appointed by Charles after the separation, who acted more like a big sister. They had a fun relationship and sometimes Harry would overstep the mark. After Diana's death, Tiggy took on the role of surrogate mother and, even though she is a wife and mother herself now, she still sees Harry whenever she can.

Harry also became close to his aunt, Diana's elder sister, Lady Sarah McCorquodale. She would regularly visit him at school. His Uncle Charles, Lord Spencer, has no role, despite his fine eulogy at Diana's funeral. In reality, with exception of his grandmother the Queen and his brother William, Harry did not really take much advice from anyone. He hated people offering advice when he hadn't even asked for it.

Charles did his best to fill the gap left by Diana's death. But it was an impossible task. She took the brave decision to free the boys from the restrictive shackles of royal protocol and Charles was determined that would continue. The tears still flowed in private moments but Diana was never coming back and both boys knew life had to carry on.

CHAPTER SIX

ETON RIFLES

Hello-hurrah there's a price to pay — to the Eton Rifles,
Hello-hurrah — I'd prefer the plague — to the Eton Rifles.
PAUL WELLER, THE JAM, LYRICS OF THE NO. 1 SINGLE
RELEASED NOVEMBER 1979

On 2 September 1998 Prince Harry arrived for his first day at Eton, following in the footsteps of his brother, Prince William. The thirteen-year-old was driven to the exclusive Berkshire school, close to Windsor Castle, the Queen's preferred residence, in a Vauxhall estate car by Prince Charles.

The two posed briefly for photographers – Harry managing an enforced smile – before entering Manor House, the place Harry was to call home, and joining his then sixteen-year-old brother as a boarder. As is tradition, they took tea with housemaster, Dr Andrew Gailey, and his wife Shauna, and the parents of other boys starting at the school, before they both went to check over Harry's room. Clearly, the young prince was a little nervous.

The photographers, as they always do, shouted his name out to get him to look straight down their lenses and, if anything, he looked a little overwrought. Wearing a light-green sports jacket, he was formally introduced to the 'Dame' of Manor House, Elisabeth Heathcote. At one poignant moment, Charles stood beside his second son as he signed the register to enrol. When his brother was photographed three years earlier he had his mother at his side. The princes earlier asked the nation to let their mother's memory rest in peace, and put an end to public mourning. The anniversary of her death until then had seemed to be commemorated with increasing mawkishness and they, like many close to the princess, felt enough was enough.

Like his older brother, Harry wore the uniform of black tailcoat, waistcoat and stiff collar, a fashion statement dating back to the nineteenth century. After passing the common entrance exam, Harry had made it clear to his father that he wanted to join his brother at Eton, the school also attended by both his maternal grandfather, the eighth Earl Spencer, and his Uncle Charles, Diana's brother, the ninth Earl Spencer. Diana, while alive, had worried that the stress of academic achievement at the world-famous school could prove to taxing for her second son. Before her death she is said to have favoured Harry's attending Radley College in Oxfordshire and Milton Abbey in Dorset. But the young prince had been adamant and, because he was born in September, he had been able to spend an extra year at his prep school, Ludgrove, to improve his academic performance and prepare him for the tough task ahead.

The *Sun* photographer and royal commentator Arthur Edwards, whose cheeky-chappy persona belied a sharp appreciation of the royal story, summed up the young prince with one of his typical remarks on television: 'He may not be the sharpest tool in the shed, but he's a good lad and has a lot to offer. He loves everything to do with the military and I can see him having a career in the army one day.'

Not for the first time, the tabloid snapper, who had made a celebrated career photographing the Royal Family and was awarded the MBE for his troubles, had hit the nail on the head. Harry certainly was not the brightest academically, but he had common sense, he was brave and passionate and they were character traits he would call upon time and time again in his future. His former bodyguard Ken Wharfe recalled, 'Harry was a tough little chap as a boy. When we had play fights at Kensington Palace or Highgrove, he was always the one who would fight dirty. You had to watch yourself. He didn't think twice about hitting you hard where it really hurts. Saying that, Harry would be the one you would want at your side in a fight.'

At Eton, although he struggled to match his contemporaries in the classroom (but it must be said that he certainly was not as poor a student as some suggested), he excelled in sport and was to prove one of the finest military cadets the school had produced. His fearless involvement in the Wall Game, Eton College's traditional St Andrew's Day fixture described as 'brutal, open warfare' and 'utterly futile', came as no surprise to fellow pupils and games masters when he took part towards the end of his Eton career.

Harry also threw himself into his time with the cadets and there can be little doubt he would benefit from the experience later in his life.

Then seventeen years old, the emerging action man of

the Royal Family volunteered to be taken hostage by 'Taliban extremists'. In a twelve-hour ordeal, during which he was interrogated in an isolated barn, he took part in a gruelling Army cadet exercise run by the Royal Green Jackets. Harry came through with flying colours. Another participant said, 'He got glowing reports. He did exactly as a soldier should have done and didn't crack.' The prince was captured by five regular soldiers dressed as Taliban fighters, complete with Kalashnikov AK-47 assault rifles. An insider said, 'They moved him around to disorientate him, forced him to stand leaning on his finger tips against the wall and to kneel. And they shouted at him but he did exactly as he should. He said he was scared and injured to distract them and would only tell them his name, date and place of birth.' All other questions were answered with a polite, 'I am sorry but I don't have to tell you that.' Another participant said at the time, 'He had a great time he loves this sort of thing.'

Well known among his peers for his sporting prowess, as a seventeen-year-old, Harry represented the Oppidans against the Collegers, Eton's scholarship pupils, in a sport that essentially pitches an irresistible force against an immovable object: The Eton Wall Game. Bloodied noses, exhausted young men, and a nil–nil scoreline are the order of the day after an afternoon of pitched battle.

Two teams of ten players form a 'bully', or scrum, around the leather ball, and are forbidden from using their hands to free it from the mass of bodies along the 118-yard wall against which the game is played. With these ground rules, it is little wonder that there has been not a single goal in the event since before the World War One.

It was the pinnacle of Harry's sporting life at Eton. He

Above: Harry with his mother Princess Diana, and brother William, on holiday in Lech. He has always loved the excitement of outdoor adventure.

Below left: Young brothers in arms.

Below right: In 1993, aged just 9 years old, already showing a keen interest in armoured vehicles during a visit to a base in Germany.

Harry as Parade Commander of the cadet force at Eton College, where he was schooled.

Above left: Prince Harry at Clarence House, London, talking about his tour of duty in Afghanistan before his deployment, December 2007.

Above right and below: Harry sits on his camp bed in his accommodation at FOB Delhi, in Helmand province, southern Afghanistan, January 2008.

On patrol through the deserted town of Garmsir close to FOB Delhi, Southern Afghanistan, January 2008.

Above: Prince Harry mans the 50-cal. machine gun on the observation post at JTAC Hill.

Below: Sitting with a group of Gurkha soldiers after firing a machine gun.

Above: In position atop his Spartan armoured vehicle in the bright midday sun.

Below left: A signpost made by soldiers reminding them of the distance they are from home stands in FOB Dwyer, in Helmand province.

Below right: Harry shares out breakfast rations with other soldiers at dawn.

Above: Harry talks to the pilot of an aircraft operating over Afghanistan from JTAC Hill.

Below: Eating a meal under the turret of his Spartan armoured vehicle in the desert.

Above: Harry and the driver of his vehicle push start an abandoned motorcycle ridden by Lance Cpl Steve 'Geri' Halliwell, February 2008.

Below: Enjoying an early morning kick-about.

played football and rugby – as a flanker – and was also an accomplished member of the Eton polo team that emerged victorious at the National Schools Polo Championships. But Harry's selection for the Oppidans came after his sterling efforts in the 'Field Game', played by every Eton pupil from the age of thirteen. Like the Wall Game, it relied on the sole use of the feet, with no handling permitted, played on a pitch equivalent in size to a soccer or rugby field.

Like the Wall Game, the Field Game is a sport peculiar to Eton, with the first set of rules drawn up in 1847, almost twenty years before the formation of association football. It is believed that association football broke away to rid the game of the 'bully', in order to create a faster game that could be dominated by the more skilful dribblers. Despite minor rule changes, the Field Game survives today in much the same format it began with more than 150 years ago. It is a combination of 'bully' power and dribbling skills.

The Wall Game, cited as the inspiration behind quidditch in J K Rowling's brilliant *Harry Potter* novels, whose infringements including 'furking' (the use of hands in the bully), 'sneaking' (offside) and 'knuckling' (the illegal bending of an opponent's wrist while pushing his face into the wall), was certainly character-building for the young prince.

Michael Grenier, master-in-charge of Eton College's games programme, and head of the Wall Game and the Field Game, said that after hearing of Harry's involvement he was inundated with calls asking for explanations of the rules of the college's rarefied pursuits. Grenier explained, 'Although the traditional sports are still played, over the last five years there has been more of a demand from the pupils to play games against other schools, and hockey is now also a major sport. The school is branching out into more mainstream sports.'

This was all positive stuff. But Harry's teenage years were marred by a series of scandals that led the media to dub him, perhaps unfairly, a royal rebel who was out of control. His wilder, carefree side, which had proved endearing when he was a child and manifested itself in a series of sometimes hilarious pranks, took on a more worrying form in his teenage years. The Eton schoolboy found himself the star of a series of tabloid revelations about excessive drinking and drug-taking.

Allegations in 2002 prompted a media maelstrom of criticism involving not just Harry's own culpability but also the role of his father in bringing up a boy who had lost his mother at an extremely vulnerable age. The story was exclusively revealed by the *News of the World*'s infamous royalty editor Clive Goodman. Goodman's sensational story made world news. It even made the front page of the *Times of India*, which reported,

Yet another scandal has engulfed and embarrassed the British Royal Family with the revelation that one of its youngest members, Prince Harry, the 17-year-old son of Prince Charles and the late Diana, had been taking drugs, drinking himself into a stupor and was sent to a rehabilitation clinic amid stories of 'wild' parties, late-night drinking sessions, spliffs, cannabis-stoned bad behaviour and a willing cast of eager young women. Harry, third in line to the British throne, admitted to his father that he was drinking in excess and smoking cannabis. A palace spokesman confirmed that the boy, who was 16 at the time, spent much of his school holidays last year getting drunk at a country pub. The spokesman said it was a 'serious matter [but it] is now closed'.

It was enough to make the Queen cringe with embarrassment. Charles knew he had to take decisive action, not only for his son's sake but his own. His advisers told him he had to appear to be in control of the situation, as the finger of blame was pointing firmly at him for what was perceived to be his neglect of his vulnerable teenage boy in the aftermath of Diana's death.

The echoes of 'it wouldn't have happened if Diana were alive' were ringing in his famously large ears.

The triumphant Goodman, who had learned his trade alongside that brilliant gossip columnist, the *Daily Mail*'s Nigel Dempster, revealed how Harry, when home from school, had finished off his 'wild' parties in a specially converted section of the royal cellars of his father's country home, Highgrove, which the teenager had christened 'Club H'. His hideaway was equipped with a well-stocked bar and a state-of-the-art sound system.

A regular at the Rattlebone Inn, Gloucestershire, a favourite of Harry's, was quoted as saying, 'There were wild times with Harry here ... a lot of young girls from villages round here would try to catch his eye. I've seen him crawl out of barns covered in straw, brushing his hair.'

Undercover reporters claimed the pub was 'a hive of activity for drug deals and users'. When *News of the World* reporters visited the pub they reportedly found cannabis joints smoked openly at the bar. The newspaper claimed that anyone wanting more privacy, sometimes for drug-taking and selling, used the shack in the pub's back garden.

The newspaper claimed to have spoken to one dealer who had rubbed shoulders with Prince Harry. It quoted twenty-nine-year-old John Holland as saying, 'Do you want some weed or coke? I get it for personal use but I help people out. I've got plenty of weed if you fancy a smoke. It's £20 worth. It smokes all right. I can get coke for £30 a gram, but that's effort. I have to go to Shoreditch in London. It's worth the drive though. I got some for New Year's Eve, kept myself a wrap and sold the rest on.'

It was a PR disaster for the royals and Charles's then spin-doctor-in-chief, the sometimes brilliant Mark Bolland, did his best to negotiate with the *News of the World* in a damage-limitation exercise. It was leaked that Charles reacted to the news by taking his son to a drugs rehabilitation clinic to meet hard-core heroin addicts and hear horror stories about drug addiction. Bill Puddicombe, chief executive of the Phoenix House alcohol and drugs rehabilitation charity, which ran the south London clinic Featherstone Lodge, said he was surprised to discover the background behind the visit. 'I suppose I'm a little shocked. But I think it's for every parent to find a way of explaining to their teenage sons and daughters what the consequences of drug-taking can be.'

He said that Harry spent most of his visit talking with recovering heroin and cocaine addicts. 'He sat in groups with people. They explained to him what sort of experiences they'd been through, what a misery their life had been as a result of the drugs they had been taking.

'He was certainly taken aback by some of the things that he heard. Some of the things he heard would have been quite harrowing, I guess, because people have had some very difficult experiences. I'm sure he went away and he thought very deeply about what he'd seen, but at the time he was taking everything in,' he said.

After news of the visit had been announced, the Queen took the rare step of ordering a statement to be issued after Charles asked for her support.

The Palace statement read, 'The Queen shares the Prince of Wales's views on the seriousness of Prince Harry's behaviour and supports the action taken. She hopes the matter can now be considered as closed.'

Charles, who reportedly discovered a year earlier that Harry, then aged sixteen, had smoked cannabis at Highgrove, was caught in a maelstrom of criticism. He was accused of being selfish, of neglect; even his relationship with Camilla Parker Bowles was blamed. After all, had her son Tom, Charles's godson, been caught taking drugs too? The press criticism was unrelenting and not for the first time the Establishment rallied round to support Charles in his hour of need. The fact that Harry's habits on smoking made him much like many British teenagers – not least the sons of then Prime Minister Tony Blair and Foreign Secretary Jack Straw – did not put newspapers off the scent of a royal scandal.

A spokesman for Prince Charles declined to confirm details of the report, saying only, 'This is a serious matter, which was resolved within the family and is now in the past and closed.'

Blair – whose own teenage son Euan was reprimanded by police for being drunk in London's entertainment district in July 2000 – got involved, too. He said the Royal Family had handled the situation 'absolutely right'. 'They have done it in a very responsible and, as you would expect, a very sensitive way for their child,' he said on BBC television. 'It is a very difficult situation ... Well, I know this myself.'

Later, palace officials tried to make the best of the situation. They declared with puffed-up confidence that Harry was a reformed character and it was reported that he was busy preparing to go to university. But for the Queen it was a scandal too far, and she and Charles – along with the Duke of Edinburgh – agonised over the best way to keep Harry in check. Prince Philip was in no doubt that the boy needed a career in the services, preferably with the 'senior service', the Royal Navy, and the sooner the better.

The revelations shocked many in Britain and undoubtedly embarrassed the Royal Family, who had been trying to overcome decades of sensationally bad news about love affairs, marital breakdowns and topless cavorting. The story also refocused attention on the so-called 'dysfunctional' aspects of the Royal Family, with commentators remarking on the apparent inability of the Queen's children and grandchildren to get married quietly, stay married without a rash of salacious news stories across the front pages, and raise 'normal' offspring.

The acerbic Peter Mckay wrote in the *Daily Mail*,

Prince Charles's method of dealing with the errant Prince Harry is agonisingly correct – but was it sensible? Personally I'd have been happier to read that he'd given Harry a right royal roasting, reminded him of his privileged position and then taken strong measures to tighten up his son's private life and friendships. Futile, maybe, but better than the New Agey concept of visiting Featherstone Lodge rehabilitation unit in Peckham.

Was Charles over-concerned about how he would be seen in the light of Harry's misbehaviour? Perhaps so. Certainly he was well rewarded for his candour by the newspaper which first carried the 'Harry's drugs shame' story. The *News of the World* editorial comment, headlined 'Courage of a wise and loving dad', concluded: 'As a shining and enviable example of wisdom among the Windsors, he emerges as a modern King in the making.' Talk about snatching victory from the jaws of defeat.

Quite. Mckay, a respected Fleet Street veteran, was not fooled by the skilled spin of the palace and Bolland's behind-the-scenes antics. Nor was the erudite *Guardian* writer Ros Coward in an article entitled 'The trouble with Harry'. She took no prisoners either when she wrote,

The revelations about Prince Harry's drinking and cannabis use are a clear reminder of the Royal Family's principal function: to live out in the spotlight the dilemmas of ordinary families. This is why, after the death of Diana, republican sentiment faded away. Her legacy was to make us want to see what happens to the remaining characters, and use them to reflect on our own dilemmas and difficulties. Getting rid of them would be like pulling the plug on *EastEnders*. There is a huge effort to suppress this speculation. The palace is busy slamming the door on this story and most of the newspapers appear to be acquiescing. According to them, Prince Charles has dealt with the situation firmly 'but wisely'. He's taken Harry to visit a rehabilitation unit. The young prince has seen the folly of his ways and will never abuse a substance again in his life. As if. Harry's behaviour will be all too recognisable for parents of teenage males and they'll know that there's no once-off effective strategy for dealing with it. So we shouldn't accept the palace's spin about Charles's parenting. However privileged and obnoxious Harry's behaviour sounds, he has the exact profile of an adolescent who might be using substances to deal with complex and painful feelings. His early childhood was overshadowed by a hostile, mad divorce; his mother died in the worst circumstances imaginable and he was left in the care of the person who, unconsciously at the very least, he must believe caused his mother the most misery. Of course Prince Harry's privacy should be respected, but that shouldn't prevent his problems opening up a discussion about drugs, adolescent behaviour and emotional pain. It would be a shame if palace spin stood in the way of an opportunity to develop a more sophisticated understanding of young people's emotional lives and behaviour.

Radio chat-show hosts, Internet message boards and some other newspaper columnists, however, sympathised with the teenage prince, who they said must have been acutely affected by the loss of Diana and the messy and public break-up of Charles and Diana's sham 'fairytale' marriage. Analysts said the revelations about Harry had come as something of a circulation-boosting bombshell for the widely read Murdoch-owned tabloid, the *News of the World*, which ran seven pages with the screaming headline 'Harry's drug shame'. It was the first time a newspaper had broken the informal embargo that kept news of the dashing young princes out of the tabloids, unless cleared by the palace, since the death of Diana. Now that the genie was out of the bottle, many, including the royals themselves, feared a stream of salacious revelations about the young princes and their youthful indiscretions.

But what worried some senior figures at the palace was that the intrusive coverage was sanctioned by advisers around his father, notably Mark Bolland – who was not trusted by the old guard despite on the surface batting for their side. They believed that, by dealing with the devil (the media) to protect Prince Charles's already severely damaged reputation, he was betraying the vulnerable teenage prince, who should have been able to count on him for support. Bolland, perhaps, felt it was Charles – who, after all, paid his considerable wage – who needed protecting.

Also, securing a so-called 'guarantee' from the powerful tabloid that the young prince was safe in the immediate future from further attempted exposés should be considered a victory in the circumstances. Some palace insiders smelled a rat when the newspaper's decision to publish was backed by the Press Complaints Commission, the newspaper industry's self-regulating body, whose director was the respected Guy Black, who was also Bolland's life partner.

The PCC, which always stated that it regarded the protection of children's privacy as a priority, chose on this occasion to back the tabloid. It declared the Harry drugs story not just in order, but rather splendid. Black said, 'St James's Palace [Charles's private office] rightly recognised that there were important matters of public interest involved here. There was no issue to be raised in respect of privacy.'

His comment raised serious questions about why the

PCC – which was not supposed to intervene unless asked to do so by a complainant – was handing out get-out-of-jail-free cards to tabloid newspaper editors. Was it really part of his job to praise St James's Palace? And what about the privacy of other boys mentioned in the story? The broadsheet media were not happy. In an editorial comment, the *Daily Telegraph* sniffed,

> We cannot fully account for the PCC's strange behaviour, but there is a highly unusual power nexus shaping tabloid coverage of the Royal Family.
>
> Mark Bolland is the Prince of Wales's deputy private secretary, responsible for media handling. He used to be director of the PCC, and he lives with the current director, Mr Black. Both of these men are close to Rebekah Wade, editor of the *News of the World*, and her boyfriend, so close that the four of them went on holiday together last year. Surely it is not appropriate for the director of the PCC to holiday with the editor of any paper, particularly one which has run so many contentious royal stories, or for a senior employee of Prince Charles to do so, for the same reason? It would be a good idea if Lord Wakeham, the PCC's £156,000-a-year part-time chairman, were to consider the influence of this group. Someone in authority must speak out against this dangerous trend of packaging royal stories with PCC approval. It is a highly dubious practice and does nothing to protect the privacy of the young princes.

In fact so deep was the impact on Prince Charles that he took the almost unprecedented step, at least for him, of cutting back on official engagements so that he could spend more time with his son. For any parent, this would have been a concern if their teenage was behaving badly, but Charles also had to concede that he may not have spent as much time with his son as he should have. After the revelations, Harry travelled home from Eton to Highgrove to spend every Sunday with his father. It gave them both the chance for a period of quiet reflection together and helped them rebuild a relationship that had suffered through neglect. Harry was only seventeen at the time, and the fact that he was suddenly on the front pages of the newspapers made this a difficult period for him.

At the time he was exposed, royal aides privately pointed the finger at James Mulholland, a member of Harry and William's circle of friends, which forced the then twenty-four year-old to issue statement designed to clear his name. At the time he said, 'It is quite wrong to suggest I ever attended a party at Highgrove at which cannabis was smoked by anyone at all. From my limited experience, Harry is a genuinely decent chap who simply does not deserve all this.'

One can only imagine the impact that such constant negative publicity must have had on the young prince, but there were some clues. Until this point it had seemed as if Harry had many, many friends but he was discovering that in his hour of need he did not have quite as many as he thought. One could hear the sound of front doors slamming in grand country houses as respectable parents sought to avoid any guilt by association sticking to their precious offspring.

Much as the Royal Family would have liked to draw a discreet veil over the affair, there were still going to be repercussions, and not just in bad publicity. The *Sun* later reported that Harry's hopes of becoming a prefect at Eton College had been dashed over the scandal. Harry, then seventeen, had set his heart on being elected as one of the twelve elite pupils, like brother Prince William. But, although his name was one of fifty considered by a committee of outgoing prefects, the older boys decided not to vote him onto their shortlist.

The newspaper quoted a senior Eton source as saying, 'The criteria to be picked is that you must be popular, responsible and of mature character. William was extremely popular and a deserving choice. Harry's also popular. But basically he is seen to be of a different calibre, a bit of a naughty boy.'

Eton prefects, known as 'poppers', belong to the Eton Society, Britain's supposedly coolest schoolboy group. They enjoy extra privileges and are allowed to swap drab school waistcoats for their own multicoloured designs. Their duties involve helping masters keep the other 1,300 boys in check and they have the power to fine pupils who misbehave.

Prince Harry's name had been put forward by his housemaster Andrew Gailey and his exclusion was a setback for the young prince, who had set his heart on being one of the twelve. 'But there is a stigma attached to his name over the drugs business,' said the newspaper's editorial. 'Also, one of his duties would be to catch Eton boys breaking rules by slipping out to drink in pubs illegally. It would be highly hypocritical for Harry.' The decision also avoided embarrassing headmaster John Lewis, who had the power to veto any of the boys' unsuitable choices.

And, quite apart from losing the prospect of becoming a

prefect, there was the small matter of possible police involvement. The events took place in the summer at their Gloucestershire Highgrove estate and at the Rattlebone Inn in neighbouring Wiltshire, when Harry was sixteen, and his father and elder brother were both away from home. The Wiltshire Constabulary insisted at the time that the prince would not be treated any differently from other young people. While drinking below the age of eighteen and possession of cannabis were both offences, the priority was prevention rather than punishment.

Harry, perhaps for the first time since his mother's death, had become a global talking point. But not everyone took it as seriously as the British. The royal drugs scandal – if that was what it was – 'amused' the United States press, according to respected London correspondent T R Reid of the *Washington Post*.

'It's not often that I open the *News of the World* and find material for my newspaper,' he wrote, and continued,

For some reason, the editors back in Washington don't generally get excited about 'I Shagged 6 Man U Hunks' and similar *NoW* splashes. But this Sunday, when I saw the headline 'Harry's Drug Shame pages 2, 3, 4, 5, 6, 7', I knew I had a story. As an American, I'm happy my country doesn't have a monarchy. But as a London correspondent who sometimes needs a story on a sleepy Sunday morning, I'm sure glad the British do. For Americans, just as for the Brits, the Royals are a regular source of entertainment. Not that we cover these stories the same way. The British press switched into full-scale wretched-excess mode for the Prince Harry revelation; I particularly admired the way four different papers each managed to label their stories 'Exclusive!' American papers were more relaxed, and focused on two points. First, we marveled at the press coverage, wondering why a 16-year-old boy experimenting with alcohol and marijuana should be front-page news. Second, we were fascinated with the idea that Prince Charles sent his son to a rehab clinic to scare him away from drugs. American reporters here rarely get access to Charles; that may help explain his rotten press in the US. In my country, the heir to the British throne is known either as the rat who broke the heart of a beloved princess, or as a luddite who talks to his carrot plants and won't let Britain import perfectly safe genetic hybrids from American farms. For the US papers, though, Harry's wild summer was more a media story than anything else. It demonstrated once again the basic bargain involved in being a British royal these days. Just for being born right, you get the lavish palace, the long yacht, and the loyal retainers. In return, your foibles fill the tabloids on sleepy Sunday mornings.

Within a few weeks, the scandal, as if by magic, abated. Harry was back at school, protected from further media intrusion, and dreaming not of university like many of his fellow pupils, but fulfilling his life's ambition of joining the British Army

CHAPTER SEVEN

SCHOOL'S OUT

'Education is not the filling of a pail,
but the lighting of a fire.'
<small>WILLIAM BUTLER YEATS</small>

Like many of his fellow students, the young student's evident relief at finally completing his punishing schedule of tests showed in the slight swagger as he left the exam hall. It was not that he was arrogant about the quality of the work he had submitted; just that he was having trouble hiding his delight that the ordeal was finally over.

As he walked past the waiting photographers penned in behind steel barriers, he flashed a grin, clenched his fist, punched the air and declared, 'At last!' He had just finished his last A-level paper, was thrilled at the prospect of ending his school days and didn't care who knew. He went straight to his study bedroom at Manor House, which had been his sanctuary, packed the detritus of five years' student living – including a cherished black-and-white portrait of Diana that he kept on his desk – into two black bin liners and left the college for the last time. Dressed in casual blue shirt, grey jacket and beige chinos, he said goodbye to his housemaster, Dr Andrew Gailey, in front of a large crowd of photographers and younger Etonians who gathered to 'see Wales off'. There were a few cheers as he was then driven by a police protection officer in a Land Rover to his father's Gloucestershire home, Highgrove. It was 12 June 2003 and Prince Harry was now officially an Old Etonian.

The spin machine of the Royal Family was soon active again and within hours of his departure his father's office at St James's Palace announced that Harry was expected to become the first senior royal for more than forty years to join the British Army. He would be applying, they said, to the Royal Military College at Sandhurst and would undergo an assessment by the Regular Commissions Board (RCB) at Westbury, Wiltshire, at some time during his gap year. If he was accepted, the statement added, Harry would become the first senior royal to join the army since 1961, when Prince Michael of Kent, the Queen's first cousin and grandson of King George V, attended the world-famous academy, founded in 1947. Sandhurst's most recent royal graduate had been the Earl of Ulster, eldest son of the Duke and Duchess of Gloucester, who became a career officer in the King's Royal Hussars and served in Kosovo. Previous recruits also included the late King Hussein of Jordan, his son, the present King Abdullah, and the late Dodi Fayed, Diana's last love, with whom Harry had shared a holiday and who died alongside his mother in the 1997 Paris car crash.

Harry had no idea which regiment he would like to serve with, nor the length of his commission. He just knew it was what he wanted to do. It had always been his ambition. The announcement marked a significant break with royal tradition, which dictated that second sons of an heir apparent were destined for the Royal Navy. George V, George VI and his uncle Prince Andrew, Duke of York, had all followed this course. Traditionally, it was noted, senior royals had been discouraged from serving in the army, as it is deemed on the face of it more risky than other branches of the armed services. But a palace spokesman explained that Harry had 'wanted to join the army for quite some time'.

It was presented as a *fait accompli*. But, before any of these royal landmarks could be achieved, the prince needed to know that he had passed both his A-levels, in art and geography, before he would be accepted at Sandhurst. In fact, he needed attain a minimum combined score of 140 points to satisfy the basic paper entrance qualifications. He had dropped history of art the previous year so he could concentrate on getting the necessary grades for him to fulfil his dream. After that he had to attend a pre-RCB at the Royal Military Academy, which would involve physical and psychological challenges to ascertain his suitability. Only once he had passed would he be put before the full RCB at the end of his gap year. And that would be no pushover, either, entailing three days of tests during which his leadership potential and physical capabilities were assessed.

St James's Palace officials were keen to leave nobody in any doubt about Harry's suitability for his chosen career. The palace PR team made much of his success in the Combined Cadet Corps (CCF) and his prowess at sport. In his final year, he was house captain of games and also enjoyed swimming and athletics. His experience in the CCF, they said, had stood him in good stead for Sandhurst.

He had, after all, been promoted to the highest rank of cadet officer in May and was runner-up for the top accolade of Sword of Honour.

Pictures were also released of him in the Eton cadet uniform he wore when he was selected as parade commander at the Eton Tattoo. 'He has clearly got leadership qualities, which is what Sandhurst is all about,' said one senior officer who watched his performance on television. The palace PR machine, it seemed, was in full swing.

All that must have seemed a long way off for the teenage prince. He had declared that his final paper in geography had been 'not too bad'.

Although the last of his exams marked the end of his formal education at Eton, Harry did not officially leave until the end of the month, and would return for a 'leavers' supper' and end-of-term parties. He formally took leave of the headmaster, Tony Little, on 3 June, when he signed the leaving book. In it, he reportedly wrote Sandhurst as his 'next stop'. Then he was presented with the traditional gift of a volume of the poetry of the eighteenth-century Old Etonian poet Thomas Grey, a brilliant writer and thinker who was offered but refused the title of Poet Laureate. Harry accepted the volume with good grace, but poetry wasn't really his bag.

Details of his gap year were not immediately made public, but officials let the press know that it was expected to involve travelling, possibly including a stint in Australia, as well as some voluntary and charity work. He had taken ten GCSEs: Latin, single science, French, English, English literature, mathematics, history, geography, art and classical civilisation. Art, his tutors said, emerged as his strongest subject, and he had developed 'an increasingly open and experimental style'. He used red deer in Windsor Great Park as inspiration for his exam pieces.

But it was his art exam that was to be the centre of yet another 'scandal' that threatened his military career the following year. Harry was growing up. His brush with scandal over drink and drugs had given him cult status and he was particularly popular with girls. His reputation as a ladies' man may have been a bit overblown but he was popular. From the moment he turned eighteen, the media were freer to report his exploits. The palace tried to argue that he was going to Sandhurst and technically he was still in full-time education and protected by the arrangement he had had with the media while he was at Eton. But editors were having none of it. Harry was news and his wayward antics helped keep circulation up.

Royal watchers busied themselves finding out about the prince's private life. They linked him with a succession of society beauties. On one evening out, Harry was spotted in a clinch with society heiress Laura Gerard-Leigh, and there were also reports of romance with pretty polo hand Jo Davies and also with TV presenter Natalie Pinkham, who was a few years his senior. It was a link that stuck, despite repeated denials of a relationship. The royal-romance rumour mill ground to a halt, for a while at least, when he started his first serious relationship with the Zimbabwe-born student Chelsy Davy.

The daughter of a wealthy game farm owner, the pretty blonde first met her prince when she was a student at the exclusive Cheltenham Ladies' College near his country home of Highgrove. Harry later visited her at home after his first trip to Lesotho, the tiny landlocked kingdom in the heart of South Africa. They started what many believed would be a short and passionate relationship. They holidayed together and exchanged love tokens.

But this was to prove stronger than the short-run relationship predicted by many. In September 2003, Harry jetted out to Australia. The Rugby World Cup was on – a tournament in which the English would emerge victorious, famously cheered on by the jubilant prince. Harry, accompanied by the unflappable press secretary Colleen Harris and his quasi-personal secretary Mark Dyer, at first put on a great show for the demanding Australian media. They wanted a piece of the prince; after all, his grandmother was their Queen, as they put it.

A photocall was arranged, and went well. He was pictured holding an Australian Akubra hat alongside zookeepers Annette Gifford and Stacey Carter as they held koalas in front of the Sydney Opera House during a visit to Taronga Zoo. He pulled funny faces when he held a spiny echidna named Spike, and all seemed well. But the prince then winced as he grappled with the animal and yelped, 'It's pretty feisty.'

A group of around sixty schoolchildren and well-wishers vied for the prince's attention, with sisters Brooke and Jessica Brims, aged seventeen and fifteen, asking him for a kiss. He turned down the request but held on to their telephone number. He didn't talk to the press, leaving that to Colleen, who said, 'He's trying to broaden his experiences and learn about life.' Asked if he would have time to go to the pub, she replied, 'It would be nice, now and again, to sample Australian hospitality – so I hope he has some fun as well as working hard.'

Palace officials hoped that in posing for the local media he could expect a tame time from the paparazzi for the rest of his stay. But the Australians were having none of it. If the prince, now nineteen, was going to spend three months working as a £100-a-week jackeroo (a trainee worker on a sheep or cattle station) in the Australian outback, they wanted pictures of that and not of Harry playing with koalas.

The exact location of the ranches he would be working on was kept a closely guarded secret. All officials would say was that he would work as a junior stockman and his duties would include rounding up livestock in thick scrub, branding animals and chores such as fencing. But that was not going to stop the Australian paparazzi. And his visit wasn't universally welcomed by a country where Republican sentiment was strong. Politicians complained about the cost of the prince's security, an extra £240,000 cost as backup for the his own close-protection team, which threatened a prickly reception while he was in Australia. Government ministers and the Australian Tourist Commission argued that the visit was worth millions of pounds in raising Australia's tourism profile.

Within weeks, what promised so much went sour. Harry got tired dodging the local media and publicly appealed to be left alone to learn about life on an Australian outback property. Colleen was forced to issue an unprecedented statement saying the prince did not want to spend his time in Australia trying to avoid the cameras. 'Learning about the farm and the jackeroo trade, that's what he wants to do, not dodge the cameras,' she said.

She issued a plea to the world's media to leave Harry in peace at Tooloombilla, a 16,000-hectare cattle property west of Injune in outback Queensland. 'We are grateful to the media for making Prince Harry's arrival in Australia and the subsequent photocall so successful,' she said in a statement to the news agency Australian Associated Press. 'As we made clear when he arrived, Harry is here on a private visit to learn about the country and to learn new trades and disciplines.'

His priority, she insisted, was the cattle property Tooloombilla station, owned by Annie and Noel Hill, a long-time friend of Princess Diana, while Mr Hill is a son of the millionaire polo star Sinclair Hill, who had coached Harry's father Prince Charles. 'He can only do this if he's allowed to live peacefully and in privacy, away from the media spotlight,' the indomitable Mrs Harris said. 'In common with all other tours that he and his brother William have undertaken in the UK and elsewhere in the Commonwealth, we would ask the media to respect that privacy and to desist from seeking to photograph him. We would be pleased if camera crews and photographers who are currently at Tooloombilla would withdraw accordingly.'

But the Aussie media were not willing to comply. There response was, in a word, 'Tough!' Queensland Premier Peter Beattie threw his not inconsiderable weight into the ring and called on the increasing horde of local and overseas media to leave Harry alone. 'I would hope that everybody, and that includes the media, give him a bit of breathing space and respects his right to some degree of privacy,' he declared.

Back home Prince Charles was growing increasingly agitated. As heir to the throne of Australia he did not want his son's gap-year visit turning into a political row, and he vented his feelings at the powerless aides, who were doing their best to keep the situation from spiralling out of control.

Harry stuck it out. It was not the first time he and the paparazzi would clash head on. But at least on this occasion he did not use his fists. It was to be Colleen's last hurrah with the royals. The first black person to be appointed to the top household post, she had already resigned a couple of months earlier as Prince Charles's press secretary, and the search for her replacement was on. Whoever got the job would know that 'Operation Harry' – improving the young prince's poor public image – would be high on the agenda. The task fell to the charismatic, softly spoken Paddy Harverson who, at 6 feet 4 inches, towered over his charges. The forty-one-year-old former army colonel's son from Manchester was given his job by Sir Michael Peat, the former accountant with a reputation for running his wing of the Royal Family like a FTSE 100 corporation.

Harverson had been press officer at Manchester United. One of his 'triumphs' had been to minimise the fallout over Sir Alex Ferguson's differences with David Beckham. The cynics wondered what lengths he would go to to paint the royals in a favourable light. The footballing incidents were to prove a walk in the park by comparison to containing Harry.

Paddy, as he insisted on being called, was introduced to journalists who report royal matters, including me, at a drinks party. He described how Ferguson had said he was jumping out of the pan and into the fire. He said he felt like a character in a film, rolling to safety from an explosion, to find himself facing a row of assassins. The 'assassins' – who also included the *News of the World*'s Clive Goodman, with whom he would later clash, leading to a court case that would have far reaching repercussions throughout the entire newspaper industry – laughed, but they were to prove Sir Alex right.

With the Australian leg of his gap year over, Harry set off on a high-profile trip to Lesotho. At the time, many said this was a mere a publicity stunt, but they were quite wrong. I accompanied the young prince on the trip as a journalist and what I witnessed at first hand was impressive. He has inherited his mother's naturalness with the downtrodden, poverty-stricken and infirm. Lesotho is a place ravaged by AIDS and Harry wanted to do something about it.

In early 2004 he flew there to help. Media attention, he knew, would raise awareness and, hopefully, much-needed cash for the tiny orphans, so he agreed to the press facility in March. I happily penned a positive article in London's *Evening Standard* under the banner headline, 'In his mother's footsteps: Harry drops playboy image as he vows to continue Diana's AIDS work'. It was wonderful, emotive stuff. Sporting a military crew cut, Harry, wearing a khaki T-shirt emblazoned with the word 'England', arrived at the orphanage on the back of a truck with a work party of Africans and his friend George Hill. They spent half an hour building a wire-mesh fence around the orphanage compound. Afterwards, Harry played with the orphans.

Then he walked hand in hand with four year-old Mutsu Potsanse, a boy who had lost both his parents to AIDS, and said he wanted to help children in Africa affected by the disease. He was genuine when he said, 'We want to help more, and we can.' He then joined a work party building fences at a remote orphanage at Mophatoo in the Mohales Hoek region about two hours outside the capital

Maseru. Incredibly, 40 per cent of Lesotho's population had HIV or AIDS.

As Harry walked with Mutsu to where they planted a tree at the orphanage, I recalled all the visits to HIV/AIDS centres I had visited with Diana. It was right and proper, I thought, that her son should take up the cause and fight for these often forgotten people. She would have been proud. When asked what he wanted to achieve by his visit, he replied, 'Recognition. Recognition for people back in England, charities back in England, that this is a country that needs help.' He added that he had been learning about the culture. 'It's fantastic. Really good fun,' he said. The people he had met were 'very happy, smiling all the time', despite the problems they faced.

The newly installed press guru Paddy Harverson couldn't get enough of it. 'He's showing a real and genuine interest in the welfare of young people in Lesotho,' he said. 'He wants to learn more about the AIDS problem and see what work is being done. By coming here he is bringing attention to the problem.' At last there would be headlines about Harry that didn't involve drinking, drugs or girls.

Harry got stuck into the task. He had joined a doctor on his daily rounds. Prince Seeiso, the brother of Lesotho's King Letsie III and Harry's mentor on the trip, had accompanied Harry and chipped in saying, 'It is genuine concern of his. He wants some role with AIDS during his stay. He is carrying on from his mother.' It was exactly what the press gang had wanted to hear. The headline was written even before we had filed our reports on our satellite phones.

Before I left, I wanted to take a closer look, along with my good friend, the internationally respected royal photographer Robin Nunn. This was, after all, not all about Harry, but about the terrible plight of the people his visit had highlighted. Driving through a village, we encountered the tragic face of Lesotho. Matseliso Homohaka, a five-year-old girl, had lost her parents and her grandparents to AIDS. She was living with her great-grandfather in their hut in the village of Matsieng, where they eked out an impoverished existence. We recorded her story in words and pictures for the *Evening Standard*. To me she was a symbol of despair. She and eighty-three-year-old Benjamin survived by growing maize on the plateau ringed by mountains on which the village stands. Their home is a stone hut, bound together by mud and topped with a straw roof. Outside is the pot in which Matseliso had learned to make simple meals.

'We look after each other,' said Mr Homohaka. 'I have taught her to cook but I cannot afford to send her to school. It is free but I cannot afford the books and uniform.' Mr Homohaka was overcome with emotion when asked about his family's loss; his great-granddaughter was just two at the time.

He said, 'They are all gone, all gone. We are all that is left of our family. One by one, they just died, like so many here. This disease has just destroyed families.' We handed over what cash we had. It was enough to buy her a uniform and books. Hopefully, going to school would keep her from the clutches of men in the kingdom who believed having sex with a virgin child would cure them of AIDS. Harry was so moved by his experience that he set up an AIDS charity to help the orphans called Sentebale (Forget Me Not) in memory of his late mother. He returned again to make a documentary, *The Forgotten Kingdom: Prince*

Harry in Lesotho, with ITN correspondent Tom Bradby, about launching Sentebale.

He was dubbed a 'retired hellraiser' and many did not take his initiative as seriously as he did. After all, how could a young man hell bent on a career in the army have the time to run a charity of this kind. They underestimated him. He insisted, 'I've always been like this – this is my side that no one gets to see.' He said he was sure his mother would have wanted him to do it. He went on, 'There's half of me that wants to say, "Right, it's now time to follow on – well as much as I can – to try to keep my mother's legacy going." But at the age of nineteen it's pretty hard work, especially as I try to be as normal as I can and have a normal life before it gets too hectic.

'I believe I've got a lot of my mother in me, basically, and I just think she'd want us to do this, me and my brother. Obviously it's not as easy for William as it is for me. I think I've got more time on my hands to be able to help. I always wanted to go to an AIDS country to carry on my mother's legacy.'

Running his fingers through his hair, he added, 'Unfortunately it's been a long time now – not for me, but for most people – since she died.' It was the first time he had referred to his late mother on film in such a personal way.

The documentary was seen as the biggest effort to date by Paddy Harverson and his team of Clarence House spin doctors to rebrand the prince. He was filmed taking presenter Bradby around a series of projects working with children. And he was shown cradling a ten-month-old baby called Liketso, who was horrifically injured when she was raped by her mother's boyfriend. It was not a question of his being 'converted', he said: this was the real him. 'I'm not gonna take a camera crew everywhere when I'm trying to help out in different countries,' he added, with a touch of irritation.

The next part of his gap years to Argentina was not such a PR success. The prince was supposed to go there to muck out polo ponies and brush up on his riding skills, but the trip turned into a fiasco when the local media claimed the prince was forced to return home early amid reports that armed guards at the Argentinian ranch where was working had foiled a plot to kidnap him. Buckingham Palace said the stories were 'irresponsible'. Reports claimed it was Harry's laddish, drunken behaviour in local bars that had led to the threat. Argentine news reports said that security guards at the gate of the complex heard shots in the early hours and had responded by firing into the air. Police said the shots came from poachers.

Of slightly more concern to police, the press reports said, was a convicted criminal's tip concerning a plot to kidnap Harry while he was out on the town. Clarence House said only that Harry stayed at the British High Commission in Buenos Aires on the night before he flew home and claimed he had always been due home at this time. Few believed this and, as he returned to Britain, again at the centre of self-inflicted scandal, he looked relaxed in a pale-blue, open-necked shirt and blue denim jeans, but made no comment to reporters as he left a VIP lounge at the airport and departed by car.

He had been expected to return just before Christmas but he came home on 26 November. One of his staff told me, 'There was nothing in this, but once you have a reputation it follows you around.' That's as maybe, but it was a reputation that he had to ditch, and fast, and the officials at Clarence House knew it.

Worse was to come. A scandal broke in October 2004 that not only threatened to embarrass the prince but threatened his chances of a military career too. He was accused of cheating in his A-levels – and without his A-levels he could not get into Sandhurst. He was devastated at the prospect.

Harverson went on the offensive on the prince's behalf, vigorously denying the claims by former Eton art teacher Sarah Forsyth, but the mud stuck. And she was not going quietly. Forsyth was taking the top public school to a tribunal, and she didn't care who got caught in the crossfire, royal or otherwise. The revelations, first made in the *News of the World*, centred on her claims that she had been asked by a senior Eton master to help with Harry's AS-level coursework, which formed 20 per cent of his art exam grade. Clarence House said, 'It is not true that Harry cheated in his exams. These are unfounded allegations by a disaffected teacher in the context of her dispute with the school.' But the more they protested, the more it seemed there was no smoke without fire. Eton weighed in, too, describing the allegations as 'absurd'. A spokesman said, 'Eton refused to give in to what appeared to be a crude attempt to embarrass the college into paying money. That is why we are determined to fight this matter in tribunal.'

Harry, whose grade B for art and D for geography had not set the world alight anyway, was left in limbo land. Worse was to come. Ms Forsyth claimed she had Harry on tape proving her claims. In the hushed tribunal court in Reading, reporters listened to muffled 'recordings' of the prince. A short, poor-quality tape, covertly recorded by the teacher, allegedly ended with Harry saying, 'It was a tiny, tiny bit. I did about a sentence of it.' She claimed this was apparently a reference to his contribution to the coursework that was eventually submitted to the exam board.

The recording had taken place on 16 May 2003, when she was questioning him about alleged assistance he was given with his coursework. She admitted she was 'very unhappy' at making the recording but felt it was the only way she could prove that her head of department condoned cheating. She also told the tribunal that it had been difficult to get Harry alone to make the recording because 'he was usually with his bodyguards'.

Forsyth's actions were bitterly criticised by Nigel Giffen, QC, representing Eton. He said, 'It is a pretty extraordinary way for any teacher to behave towards any pupil. It is a gross breach of trust and almost certainly unlawful.' On 4 July 2005, the thirty-year-old art teacher was vindicated when the tribunal ruled that she was sacked unfairly after being bullied by Eton's head of art. But it rejected her claims that she was told to do some of the prince's written work for him to help him pass AS art. And it criticised her decision to record a conversation with Harry in which she claimed he admitted this.

By now this was water under the bridge for Harry. A couple of weeks earlier, on 21 June, he paraded publicly for the first time when he joined fellow Sandhurst officer cadets as the military academy received its colours. The Queen had originally planned to present the colours – the military flag – but cancelled due to a heavy cold. The prince was among 755 cadets who stood to attention in front of the Old College building in Camberley, Surrey. Chief of the Defence Staff General Sir Michael Walker presented the colours. It had been over thirty years since the academy performed the formal ceremony.

Harry marched in step and raised his hat in three cheers to the Queen during the parade. Standing in line, second from the end in the second row from the back, the prince was spoken to by General Walker, but simply nodded in response. Addressing guests and cadets, Walker said, 'I'm sure you all wish to join me in wishing Her Majesty good speed for a rapid and full recovery.' He also read out a personal message from the Queen. It said, 'The challenges that lie ahead will test to the full your character, your physical endurance and your intellect. You will have the privilege of commanding men and women of the highest quality and that privilege demands a strong sense of responsibility and the need to set an example and to remain true to the Sandhurst motto, "Serve to Lead".'

CHAPTER EIGHT

HARRY THE NAZI?

'I am very sorry if I caused any offense or embarrassment to anyone.
It was a poor choice of costume and I apologize.'
PRINCE HARRY'S APOLOGY, JANUARY 2005.

It wasn't going too well for the young royal inside the Pangaea nightclub at the heart of London's West End. He had made a princely play for twenty-two-year-old aspiring actress Anne-Marie Mogg, but his charm offensive was getting him nowhere. Perhaps he should have tried a little harder than sending over a flunkey to do his chatting up for him while he nursed his favourite vodka and cranberry juice on a private table of aristocratic teenage girls. But the sassy and, it has to be said, rather stunning Miss Mogg was having none of it. She was wearing a low-cut white top with low-slung white jeans and sitting with her model friend Josephine. They were looking good and having fun.

It was around 2 a.m. in October 2004 and it was supposed to have been the month that Harry started his first intensive officer training at Sandhurst, but a knee injury had postponed this until May. If false accusations of cheating in his art examination course work had not been enough, two further incidents would rock his reputation and seriously threaten his army career prospects, calling into question his temperament and judgement.

The attractive model recalled, 'We were at the bar when this good-looking, well-dressed young guy came over and asked if we wanted a drink. We said, "No, thanks" and my friend started chatting to him. It was then I noticed he had two friends with him, standing further away, and one was Prince Harry.

'He smiled at me and I smiled back, but he blushed and seemed quite shy, and when he didn't try to speak to me I just carried on talking to other people I knew. Then Harry and his two friends went back over to their table, which was in the middle of the club. Everyone knows it's the best table, where all the celebrities always sit.'

Harry, who watched the girls dance provocatively, didn't give up. After a while he sent his friend over for a second attempt. And this time emphasised it was a royal request.

'He said, "Girls, Harry would like to invite you over to his table,"' Ms Mogg continued. 'Josephine repeated, "Harry?" and the friend stressed, "Harry, as in 'Prince Harry',," so there was no question who he was talking about. He kept emphasising it was Prince Harry.

'I said no. I didn't want to be seen as one of those groupie wannabes you always see at clubs, perched on tables with famous people. I don't treat anyone differently, and I wasn't going to give him any special treatment because he was a royal.'

Then his pals started cracking jokes about his inability to 'pull' the models, be he royal or otherwise. His mood became blacker. When the two models left the club there was already a posse of paparazzi waiting outside on the pavement.

A few minutes later, at around 3.30 a.m., Harry and his pals emerged along with the prince's protection officer, who had been drinking non-alcoholic drinks throughout the evening. A scuffle between Harry, his face flushed from drinking to excess, and a photographer, Chris Uncle, ensued. Harry appeared to lash out and strike him.

Mogg has come forward to shed new light on Harry's now infamous fracas with the paparazzo. She said she feared her firm rebuttal of the prince's callow advances minutes earlier may have darkened his mood – and caused him to snap when he would otherwise have dealt with the paparazzi good-naturedly. She portrayed Harry as shy and bumbling, capable of talking to the opposite sex within his own aristocratic circle, but hopeless at engaging with sassy, streetwise girls such as herself.

On not wanting to be seen as a mere groupie, Mogg said, 'Don't get me wrong, he's a very good-looking guy. He's much taller and stronger-looking than I thought from photographs. If he hadn't been a royal, I probably would have gone over.

'I think he was definitely too shy to approach us himself. It was quite sweet. He kept looking over from his table as we were dancing – but we didn't see him dance all evening. He just hung out with his friends, watching and sipping his vodka.

'They were cracking jokes. I hope they weren't teasing him about being shy. The photographers must have said stuff about us to him as well, which must have provoked him.

'When we left the club all the photographers were asking

about Harry and if we had sat at his table, so I can only imagine what they were saying to him.

'We left just before them, and as we were walking down the street we heard this massive scuffle behind us. We knew the commotion was about Harry.'

Within hours, the incident was front-page news in the respected London *Evening Standard*. Was Harry out of control? I had woken Paddy Harverson from his slumber with the news. He said he needed time to check with the protection team and within moments had done his best to turn Harry from aggressor to victim.

There was no chance, he said, of Harry's apologising to the paparazzo. 'I don't think it really requires that,' he said with assurance. Why should he apologise? After all Harry had been hit in the face with the camera; he had been attacked. The facts and the photographs of the incident didn't appear to back up the PR spin. There was, after all, not a mark on Harry yet the twenty-four-year-old photographer, Chris Uncle, suffered a cut lip and insisted he had been struck without provocation.

But Harverson was having none of it. 'The fact was the paparazzi were pretty aggressive,' he told BBC radio. Fortunately for Harry, Uncle chose not press charges, despite alleging that Harry had 'deliberately lashed out' at him. Prince Charles was furious. Why had his son been placed in this invidious position? The actor Hugh Grant weighed in, backing Harry and offering him advice on how to deal with the paparazzi. 'I shout at them, kick them, and hate them. I've always been dreadful with them. In fact, I fantasise sometimes about leaving London to escape the paparazzi, but it's very difficult to know where to go,' he said unhelpfully.

Given the French paparazzi's alleged involvement in his

mother's death seven years earlier, people were generally sympathetic towards him. He was human, after all. They wound him up. Every young lad is entitled to have some fun. That, anyway, was the general view. But it was not a view shared by the Queen, who was growing increasingly concerned with her grandson's public displays of aggression. He was a prince, after all, not a pop star. Senior household figures agreed. The incident was a shameful echo of the binge-drinking culture ruining city centres and the palace view was that it had to change, and fast.

But, as if the fracas with a photographer had not been bad enough, Harry would be the centre of a row that had international ramifications leading to senior politicians questioning his suitability to serve as a British soldier and causing a king-size hangover for the prince and the rest of the Royal Family.

In a marquee pitched in the grounds of a country mansion owned by the Olympic triple-gold-medallist rider Richard Meade, the young and expensively educated drank, danced and flirted until 5 a.m. Harry had arrived in a jacket with the German flag on the arm and removed it to reveal the desert uniform of General Erwin Rommel's Afrika Korps, complete with the badge of the Wehrmacht on the collar, that he had hired from Maud's Cotswold Costumes, in the Gloucestershire village of Nailsworth.

According to an insider, the main reaction of other guests was, 'You're going to get into trouble for that' rather than any particular outrage, although a few did say they were 'horrified'. And no one appeared bothered by the general theme of the party itself – natives and colonials. Indeed among the Windsors the subjugation of the colonies appears to be a popular topic: at Prince William's twenty-first, guests dressed to the theme of *Out of Africa*.

The revelry continued well into the early hours. Cars started arriving at the farm around 5 a.m. and disco music could be heard pumping from behind the farm with the occasional burst on the PA system by guests talking in an upper-crust accent.

The following day, 13 January 2005, when the Beaufort Hunt met to gallop across the vales and fields of the Gloucestershire–Wiltshire borders, the hangovers of the majority of its young followers who had attended the party thrown by Meade for his three children had no doubt subsided. But the fallout from the choice of dress of one of the 250 guests had exposed the peculiar sense of humour and lack of decorum of a young royal and his upper-crust twentysomething friends. And, when the picture of the prince wearing a swastika armband was splashed across the front page of the *Sun*, all hell was let loose.

Harry was a pariah and he dived for cover. Of course, there were some who defended him. One of the guests piped up with the stock leave-Diana's-boys-alone defence, saying, 'If William and Harry want to enjoy themselves at a party, they should be able to do that in private. People should just leave them alone.' They failed to note that the person who had sold the offending picture to the *Sun* had been a guest at the party.

The betrayal was an inside job.

Within hours, Harry apologised for his lack of judgement. Clarence House issued a statement saying, 'Prince Harry has apologised for any offence or embarrassment he has caused. He realises it was a poor choice of costume.'

But some senior figures dismissed his apology as feeble.

The then-Conservative leader Michael Howard told BBC Radio 4's *Today* programme that Prince Harry should appear in person, rather than talk through a spokesman. And the Board of Deputies of British Jews said, 'It was clearly in bad taste, especially in the run-up to Holocaust Memorial Day on the 27th of this month, which the Royal Family will be taking a leading role in commemorating.'

Rabbi Dr Jonathan Romain, of the Reform Synagogues of Great Britain, said, 'The fact that the palace has issued an apology indicates that this was a mistake by the prince. But, having been given, the apology should now be accepted.'

But the California-based Simon Wiesenthal Center, one of the largest international Jewish human-rights organisations, said the prince should attend a ceremony being held at the death camp Auschwitz later that month to mark the sixtieth anniversary of its liberation. Their rebuke said that, in Auschwitz, the prince would see the results 'of the hated symbol he so foolishly and brazenly chose to wear' at the party. 'This was a shameful act, displaying insensitivity for the victims,' a statement said. 'Not just for those soldiers of his own country who gave their lives to defeat Nazism, but to the victims of the Holocaust who were the principal victims of the Nazis.'

Even the Queen's former assistant press secretary, Dickie Arbiter, who had been close to Harry's mother, could not defend her son, 'This young man has got to come upfront and be seen in person making an apology,' he said.

But the strongest condemnation, and perhaps the most significant, came from the former Armed Forces Minister Doug Henderson, who said the picture showed that the prince was 'not suitable' for the prestigious military academy at Sandhurst. 'If it was anyone else, the application wouldn't be considered,' said Henderson, who is also the Labour MP for Newcastle upon Tyne North. 'It should be withdrawn immediately.' But Prince Charles was determined his younger son would not be hung out to dry. However, he wasn't in for an easy ride either.

The damage was done. Harry was branded 'a misfit' by the influential writing duo Richard Kay and Geoffrey Levy for Middle England's 'Bible', the *Daily Mail*. They claimed that his father was rarely there for him. They claimed royal aides were too frightened to speak out for fear of losing their precious jobs. Harry was also accused of lacking common sense and self-control; perceived as a boy bent on little more than squeezing every last drop of pleasure out of his princely privilege – 'an ignorant toff', as one senior royal figure put it anxiously.

But it was Charles who came under the sharpest fire from their pens. Kay and Levy wrote,

Did anybody notice when Prince Harry changed into Nazi uniform at Highgrove for a fancy dress party? Did anyone care that he would be cavorting about in a way that would insult, and indeed upset many people?

Astonishingly, it seems not. As ever, his father Prince Charles was unaware of what his son was up to. He was far away in Scotland, perhaps deep in his usual misery over the wretchedness of his cosseted life or ruefully checking the latest bills for Mrs Parker Bowles's burgeoning wardrobe. Either way, here is a Prince who, by common consent, is something of a misfit, wilful and dangerously lacking in judgement, for whom there is no family or official mechanism watching over him.

The attention also turned on Harry's elder brother, who until now had been able to maintain a squeaky-clean image. It would have been unthinkable for the brothers not to know what each other was wearing for the party, so why had William not pulled his brother up on his choice? All around Harry were people who knew and did nothing, or did not know when they should have known.

Some former aides openly, albeit from the safety of anonymity, laid the blame squarely on Charles. 'Everyone knows that the problems are down to his father,' one said. 'However hard Charles tries to cover it up, the fact is both William and Harry have been virtually left to bring themselves up since their mother died. They have been neglected, and Harry was, frankly, too young to cope and not bright enough to pull himself together. If there had been someone – anyone – around to tell him that putting on a Nazi uniform was not the big joke he thought it was, he would have thought about it again. I can't say he would have taken it off because – as with William – he's grown up believing in his birthright. I shudder sometimes at what his mother would think if she knew what was happening to him.'

Once again, the resilient Harry rode out the storm, but his lack of judgement had placed his future superiors at Sandhurst in an awkward position. The last thing the college needed was for the public confirmation by the Ministry of Defence of Harry's guaranteed attendance at the academy to be seen as preferential treatment.

And the MoD did formally confirm that Harry's place would not be affected by his having worn the Nazi insignia at the fancy-dress party. Despite Doug Henderson's earlier comments that his place at Sandhurst should have been withdrawn – because MoD officials had stated when Harry had passed the selection test for Sandhurst that the academy would treat him exactly the same way as any other cadet – the MoD were now put in the sensitive position of being drawn into the row by having to make a comment.

They made it clear that Harry was not yet in the army and was, therefore, not subject to army rules and regulations. Colonel Bob Stewart, the former commanding officer of the Cheshire Regiment, said that he would have given Prince Harry two weeks of extra duties if he had been in the army and caught wearing Nazi uniform. An official spokesman left the prince in no doubt that, had he been an officer cadet when he was seen and photographed wearing the fancy dress, Sandhurst would have taken 'a pretty dim view' of his conduct. It was pointed out that sanctions existed for displaying such a lack of judgement, although an incident of this sort would not have led to a formal charge, such as bringing the army into disrepute.

It was yet another headache for Charles's new PR man, Paddy Harverson. And, while Harry and even Charles received some sympathy over the Nazi escapade, little of it reached Harverson. Some, prematurely, even saw it as his comeuppance. Since he had taken up his role as the head of the princes' PR, Harverson had not been universally admired. While Harry and William took warmly to the former army colonel's son, others, particularly in the media, did not. The Nazi incident was horrendous for him. He was at Clarence House when the *Sun* called him to say it had a photograph of Harry in Wehrmacht garb. He went through the moves dictated by his trade:

informing Sir Michael Peat and Prince Charles before working out an apology with Harry. To be fair, even Harverson's critics acknowledge that he inherited the problem of Harry's behaviour. One predecessor said, 'That boy is out of control.'

There was no place for 'out-of-control' trainee officers in the British Army. Harry was in for a short, sharp shock.

CHAPTER NINE

OFFICER CADET WALES

'There's no way I'm going to put myself through Sandhurst and then sit on my arse back home while my boys are out fighting for their country.'
<small>PRINCE HARRY INTERVIEWED FOR HIS TWENTY-FIRST BIRTHDAY</small>

The idea of Sandhurst training is to break you down, so that the army can 'remould' you in to the desired form, that of an officer with all the qualities needed to lead some of the finest fighting troops in the world. In Harry's case they did not so much want to reshape him as break his old mould altogether and throw the bits away.

But, even though he was aware of how tough life was about to become, he knew in his heart that the army would be the making of him, and those who doubted him because of past misdemeanours would be proved wrong.

He was under no illusion that the first five weeks were going to be tough, a total lockdown. There would be no passes to leave the academy and he and his fellow cadets would be totally isolated from the world outside. It was part of Sandhurst's regime designed to make the most absurd, mundane things take on life-threatening importance. These building blocks of military discipline, the menu for the first five weeks, were pretty basic. Boots so shiny they look like glass; creases in your trousers you could shave with and the ability to ensure you are not at the back during the company and platoon runs.

Officer Cadet Wales – Prince Harry's rank and name for his forty-four weeks of training at Sandhurst – was left in no doubt that the most important aspect of his training was not to draw attention to himself. Avoiding the unflinching eye of the colour sergeant or drill instructor was paramount. If he did, he risked punishment or humiliation.

Before he arrived on 8 May 2005 there were plenty of former Sandhurst cadets willing to offer advice to him via the media. A senior defence analyst for Janes Consultancy Group and former army Major Charles Heyman said, 'At Sandhurst, Prince Harry will be watched all the time, twenty-four hours a day, and get away with nothing. If you're told to appear at a certain time in certain dress, with certain weapons, then you do, or you are in trouble,' he told the BBC.

'He's going to see some male role models who will shock him down to his very foundations. Sandhurst brings people down to size. It's a big reality check and, the further up the pyramid you are, the bigger the shock. It will change him. I think he'll mature quite quickly after forty-four weeks at Sandhurst. They will not care that he's Prince Harry,' insisted Heyman.

That was as maybe, but once they had their first senior royal for years in their midst they milked it for all they could. The MoD PR machine went into overdrive. I was among the hordes of press invited inside the academy and given a VIP tour of the place. It was pretty impressive stuff, too. The officer cadets selected to talk to us were dynamic young people with amazing CVs and total dedication to duty. One journalist went away feeling proud to be British.

During the first five weeks of basic training, Harry's life was an endless rush of activity and attention to detail. He was left no time to recover his thoughts. If he missed his girlfriend, Chelsy, he really wouldn't have had time to think about it. Basic drill, weapons training and map reading would keep Wales and his fellow cadets running from classroom to parade ground to outdoor training. His bed would have to be made with hospital corners and the blankets folded into a bed block.

Such was the discipline of the academy. The officer training in the first five weeks is mirrored in military establishments across the country for all ranks. The only difference at Sandhurst, where the cadets come from top public schools and universities, was that for Harry and the rest of the officer cadets there was occasional leadership training, but as a rule this was further on in the course.

And so Harry, accompanied by his father, pitched up alongside 270 other recruits at the Old College training centre in Camberley, Surrey. He had brought with him his standard kit, including a pair of heavy, army-issue black boots he had been given weeks earlier to break in. He displayed no sign of nerves as he strode up to the commandant of Sandhurst, Major General Andrew Ritchie, Adjutant Major George Waters and tough-talking Sergeant Major Vince Gaunt in the leafy, neatly kept grounds. Gaunt went on record as saying that the young royal would get the same treatment as every other cadet during his officer training. There would be no special privileges for princes, and that was just how Harry wanted it.

The prince, who had delayed his admission for four

months due to a knee injury, would be put through his paces on the Royal Military Academy's gruelling commissioning course. He had spent a romantic break with his nineteen-year-old girlfriend ahead of intense course training knowing he would have no free weekends for the first five weeks.

Perhaps missing the stories of the rabble-rousing royal Harry, the *Sun* tried to generate a story of its own when it smuggled a reporter into the academy with a fake bomb to expose the lax security. Defence Secretary John Reid demanded a 'quick investigation' into what he termed a 'serious security breach'.

'There are no excuses,' he boomed. 'We ought to expect a reasonable degree of security when it comes to our armed forces. And we ought to expect a pretty good degree of security when it comes to the Royal Family, so when you put them both together things like this shouldn't happen.' The *Sun* said it had acted after being tipped off by a 'concerned insider' worried about the state of security at the academy.

My old colleague Graham Dudman, the newspaper's managing editor, said its actions were intended to 'expose, for the public interest, gaps in security'. 'What would have happened if that hadn't been the *Sun* that the source had called?' he asked. 'What if he'd called somebody far more sinister? You would have a completely different news agenda today. You wouldn't be trying to talk down the *Sun* on a fantastic piece of journalism: you'd be talking about something a whole lot more serious and dangerous. Everything about the reporter was suspect but it wasn't picked up,' he added. But, in truth, the story had more to do with the silly season – the summer period when little or nothing happens in newspaper terms – and perhaps the tabloid was missing its usual feast of rebel royal stories that followed the prince.

Harry was determined nothing would knock him off his chosen path. He had always wanted to be a soldier and he was nearly there. In an interview, arranged to mark his twenty-first birthday – celebrated while he was still a cadet – he showed he was not just doing it for the uniform or for show. One comment stood out. In a punchy interview, Harry showed there was more to him than froth, frolics and funny gags. The Sandhurst cadet became the first member of his family to declare in so many words that he did not intend to 'sit on my arse back home'.

Others may have fretted that his life had neither shape nor purpose, but Harry – who joined Prince Philip, his father and brother and his uncle Prince Andrew as a Counsellor of State, meaning that now he was twenty-one he was able to stand in for the Queen at Privy Council meetings – was clear that he was serious about an army career and his charity work among AIDS victims in Lesotho.

Harry came out fighting and defended himself over his party-prince image. 'I am who I am. I'm not going to change,' he said, although he claimed he had grown up despite his childish streak. Wearing a crumpled blue and white shirt, green khaki trousers, six metal bangles on his right wrist and a leather band on his left, Harry spoke to the Press Association, BBC Radio and Sky News at Highgrove. He left viewers in no doubt that he would be a serious career soldier.

Harry described being shouted at by regimental sergeant majors and treated like a piece of dirt. 'I know that I've been treated equally. If not, in a couple of cases maybe slightly differently in the sense that, "He is who he is, let's treat him even worse to make him feel really where he's at." It did me good.

'I do enjoy running down a ditch full of mud, firing bullets. It's the way I am. I love it.' He added, 'I've seen the way the army changes people, mostly for the good and also for the bad as well – you know, the typical army officer. I want to be an army officer and do the job, but at the same time I don't want to change that much.'

He left nobody in any doubt of his ultimate intention to serve on the frontline when he said, 'There's no way I'm going to put myself through Sandhurst and then sit on my arse back home while my boys are out fighting for their country.'

The prince also showed his maturity when, in person for the first time, he spoke of his regret over the 'Harry the Nazi' escapade. 'Looking back on it now, and at the time as well, it was a very stupid thing to do and I've learnt my lesson – simple as that, really. Maybe it was a sign of my own immaturity. That was then, this is now. I am becoming twenty-one. Something like that I will never do again. It was a stupid thing to do. I think it's part of growing up.'

The following spring, on 12 April 2006, Harry finally graduated from Sandhurst as an army officer and the joy on his face on the glorious day was clear to see. On his passing-out parade the newly installed Second Lieutenant Wales was inspected by his grandmother. The Duke of Edinburgh, Prince Charles, his stepmother the Duchess of Cornwall and his brother were also at the ceremony. The prince marched in the military college's Sovereign's Parade along with 219 officer cadets. Simultaneously, Clarence House released that Cornet Wales (his official rank) would serve in an armoured reconnaissance unit training to become a troop commander, in charge of eleven men and four light tanks, and could serve in a conflict zone. His senior officer, Major General Sebastian Roberts, said it was 'eminently possible' the young royal could find himself serving in Iraq or Afghanistan. Tradition dictated that the pips on his shoulder – one star signalling his rank – remain covered up until midnight at the Sandhurst ball. It promised to be quite a night. His girlfriend Chelsy had flown into Heathrow especially for the occasion, but stayed away from the ceremony to avoid upstaging her soldier-prince.

But before the revelries the newly appointed army officer had his official duties to fulfil. The Queen found her grandson without any trouble when she reviewed the lines of officer cadets. She gave Prince Harry a broad smile. His cheeks appeared to redden, possibly in anticipation of being ribbed later by the cadets next to him who were not selected for a chat with their sovereign. He also grinned – apparently not a breach of military etiquette.

In glorious sunshine, the prince passed out at Sandhurst with a one-off salute from his older brother, Prince William, a moment he apparently enjoyed but had better not get used to. Sandhurst had never seen so many photographers lining up to snap Harry, his family and his guests. It was a proud moment for them all. He had completed the final ceremony after his forty-four-week course and emerged with an exemplary record, proving the detractors all wrong. Alone among the officer cadets, he was wearing on his chest a vigorously polished Jubilee Medal. Others in the armed forces had to have served for five years to be eligible for the medal honouring the

Queen's Jubilee. Moments later, Harry saluted in unison with his brother as they both bade farewell to the Queen and the Duke of Edinburgh after a formal lunch in the dining hall of Old College.

A fanfare greeted the arrival of the prince's grandparents – it was the first time the Queen had attended the Sovereign's Parade in fifteen years. She and Prince Philip sat in gold-coloured seats on the royal dais, facing the imposing Old College building, about 50 feet from their grandson. 'This is a very special occasion for me, as it is for all of you who are gaining your commissions today,' she said in an address to the senior cadets.

The Queen, in a tan coat, was accompanied on the reviewing dais by the Duke, the Sandhurst commandant Major General Andrew Ritchie and his wife, another Camilla, dressed in yellow. Charles and *his* Camilla, dressed in dark purply blue, sat in the front seats to the left of the dais. They sat next to the head of the British armed forces, General Sir Mike Jackson, in the VIP seats. Among his guests in the main stand was Harry's former nanny Tiggy Legge-Bourke (now Pettifer, since her marriage in 1999), who had cherished him so dearly in the months after his mother's death and was now there to support him.

Harry, a trust-fund millionaire several times over in his own right, was now earning £60.11p a day, equating to £21,940 a year as a second lieutenant in the Blues and Royals, one half of the Household Cavalry. He marched unexceptionally during the hour-long ceremony. By contrast, some of his Sandhurst mates were so bent backwards with chins up that they appeared on the verge of falling.

There were no dramas to note, apart from perhaps the

odd wayward movement of Winston, the white horse being ridden by Major Stephen Segrave, the academy adjutant and Irish Guards officer who commanded the parade. Segrave ended the ceremony by riding Winston up the steps of Old College. Minutes earlier, the officer cadets, including twenty-three women and sixteen overseas cadets, had marched up the steps as the Coldstream Guards band played 'Auld Lang Syne'. As they did so, they changed from officer cadets to second lieutenants – the official passing-out.

For forty-four weeks – with a few notable exceptions and a trip a week earlier to a local lap-dancing bar – Harry had played the perfect trainee officer. Now, he was officially allowed to let his hair down at a party at the graduation ball. And Chelsy was determined not to let her man down. She must have known the moment she tried on her new slinky gown that she would be the belle of the ball. A sheath of turquoise satin, it clung in all the right places, skimming lightly over her hips, scooping low at the back and flowing, mermaid-like, to the floor. She was dazzling, and knew it. Chelsy Davy was always going to draw looks when she attended Harry's passing-out ball, but dressed in this gown, with her hair pinned up, elongating her neck and tanned back, she did more than that. Whether she was standing aside while Harry posed for photographs with his brother officers – or, more often, their female guests – or kissing him passionately on the dance floor she stole the show.

She had spent the afternoon at the hairdresser's before pouring herself into what she had informed friends was a 'show-stopping' dress. One guest said afterwards, 'She looked absolutely stunning. Her dress was amazing. There must have been two thousand people there but you couldn't help looking at her wherever she was, which was usually by Harry's side. They were happy to talk to other people but weren't really hanging out with anybody but each other. They were very much there as a couple, while most other people were part of bigger groups.'

Although each cadet is allowed to invite nine guests to the day and evening celebrations, the only guests to join Harry in the evening were Chelsy and his brother. Prince William's girlfriend, Kate Middleton, had been expected to attend but did not.

Not that Harry's spirits were dampened. He had a whale of a time. 'He was excited, like all the cadets,' said the guest. 'The atmosphere on the night, once the ceremony is over and the champagne corks start popping, is incredible. I thought it would be really formal and stiff, considering it's black-tie and military, but it was nothing of the sort.'

The evening was a chaotic mixture of great tradition and surprising informality. There was no sit-down meal. Instead, officer cadets proudly wore their £2,000 tailored mess suits for the first time as they ate hamburgers from a van parked in the grounds. Onion rings were washed down with champagne. And the usually immaculate site was turned into something resembling a travelling fairground, with dodgems and other attractions hired for the occasion.

The evening began at 7.30, when cadets and their guests had drinks with their platoons. Beer, wine, champagne, gin and vodka were served freely as videos of each cadet's 'highlights' were played to raucous applause and laughter. At 9.30 p.m., the guests converged on the college gymnasium, which had been breathtakingly transformed for the evening. Covered walkways linked a series of rooms. In one, a live band played in front of a chequered dance floor, surrounded by high tables, uplit in red. In another there was jazz. Elsewhere, guests could play roulette or blackjack in a casino, drink vodka from an ice bar or eat from a chocolate fountain.

In another room, scenes from the day's parade were played on large screens. One partygoer said, 'The music was pretty cheesy in the band room. But it got everybody up dancing and singing. He was joking with other cadets and is obviously very popular.'

Harry was happy to talk to anybody who approached him, though he did seem keener to talk to the girls.' At one point an excited female guest asked Harry to pose with her for a photograph. He obliged and, turning to walk away, winked at his bodyguard and mouthed, 'Phwoar, she's hot.' Even with his girlfriend in earshot, Harry was still Harry.

Plenty of girls wanted to get close to him and it didn't matter to them that Chelsy was there. At one point a group of four or so girls, who were quite drunk, dared one of their friends to pinch Harry's bum. Instead of being annoyed, Harry just pinched her bum back and she ran off giggling.

But it was a bit of fun. He spent most of the night kissing Chelsy, drinking and smoking. 'Harry was very much there with Chelsy,' said one guest. They were kissing passionately, hugging and holding hands, massively and openly affectionate.' Just before midnight the guests rushed outside for a spectacular fireworks display. Then, to applause and shouting, the cadets tore off the velvet strips that had been covering the officers' pips on their suits. When he and his brother officers went back to the gymnasium they were met with a terrific 'Congratulations!'

Harry Wales, may have been a prince of the realm, but at last he was a proper soldier an officer in the British Army by right.

CHAPTER TEN

BANNED FROM IRAQ

'There have been a number of specific threats, some reported, some not
reported, which relate directly to Prince Harry as an individual.
These threats expose not only him but also those around him to a degree
of risk that I now deem unacceptable.'
GENERAL SIR RICHARD DANNATT, MAY 2005

Perhaps it wasn't meant as a loaded question but that didn't mean Harry couldn't see the catch. After all, he had lived with the lies and innuendo about his paternity for years. John Bingham, then chief reporter of the Press Association, sent out to Afghanistan to interview Prince Harry in January 2008, tossed it into the mix, anyway. Knowing John, he probably meant it innocently enough, but, judging by Harry's reaction, he wasn't prepared to leave it open-ended. He knew what the tabloids were like. Even if the reporters were thousands of miles away back in London, he knew an ill-chosen word or two on the PA newswire could come back and bite.

'What is the attraction for you in the army?' John asked innocently enough. 'We all remember the picture of you aged eight ... Is it in the DNA?'

The prince, by now hardened to life as a soldier in lawless Helmand Province, southern Afghanistan, looked him squarely in the eyes, paused for a second or two before giving an answer that left no room for misunderstanding. 'Clearly not, because my father was in the navy,' he replied.

Maybe John was referring to the military prowess of so many of Harry's regal ancestors – the aforementioned kings and princes who have ridden into battle leading their men from the front. But Harry was not taking any chances. Throughout his young life, the prince had been dogged by cruel and preposterous stories suggesting his real father was not Prince Charles but the man his late mother publicly said she 'loved and adored', Major James Hewitt. Hewitt had been close to Harry. In fact, the prince had idolised him as a boy, not knowing of course at the time that his mother and the dashing red-headed Household Cavalry officer shared a bed while his father was away.

Hewitt was everything Charles wasn't. Diana certainly fell for him, and so did her sons. The princess was hopelessly in love with the handsome soldier and when her marriage had reached its lowest ebb he was her salvation. He provided the passion and support as no other man ever could during their five-year relationship. If she had been anybody other than the Princess of Wales, she would have probably left her older husband and married the man to whom she was eminently more suited. And, despite his ultimate betrayal, throughout their long-running affair he was discreet and trustworthy.

To William, and particularly Harry, he was a good mentor, somebody the wannabe soldier could look up to. After all, he was a war hero, a real-life tank commander in the First Gulf War. In many ways, he was just what the little Prince Harry wanted to be. Ken Wharfe, Diana's protection officer, guarded the princess throughout her affair with Hewitt in the late 1980s and early 1990s. He said he always liked Hewitt as a man and thought he was good for the princess and for her sons. 'I was not there to judge the princess's behaviour. Yes, she was involved in an adulterous relationship, which, given who she was, could have been deemed treason,' he said.

'But, thankfully, this was not Tudor England, otherwise she may have had her head chopped off like Henry VIII's queens, Anne Boleyn or her cousin Katherine Howard. As Prince Charles was enjoying his own extramarital relationship with Camilla, it would hardly have been fair. I was just there to keep her safe, so for him to criticise her behaviour would have been hypocritical in the extreme.'

Ken added, 'James made the princess very happy and that made the lives of everyone around her better, and that included her two boys. They didn't know that their mother was sleeping with James – as lovers they were always very discreet and careful not to upset the children, especially when they stayed at Highgrove when the Prince of Wales was away.'

When he was first introduced to Diana, Hewitt offered to be her riding instructor and gave her renewed confidence as a horsewoman. He also taught her sons to be accomplished little horsemen, great preparation for the cavalry officers they would one day become. Harry, perhaps more than his older brother, simply adored Hewitt.

'It was James this and James that, every five minutes,' said another member of staff who worked for the princess at the time. 'But it's a hell of leap to say James was his father. People can be so cruel. They may have had the same hair colouring but that was about as far as it went,' she said.

Dickie Arbiter – Diana's accomplished press secretary – and Ken Wharfe have both dismissed the claims publicly. Arbiter summed it up perfectly: 'To be blunt the dates don't add up. The princess hadn't even met James Hewitt when Prince Harry was born. Enough said.'

Wharfe insisted the princess told him personally that the prince was the father. 'I remember her telling me that she didn't know how Harry had been conceived because at the time he [the prince] had already gone back to his lady [Camilla], but she said that the Prince of Wales was the father. The malicious rumours that still persist about the paternity of Prince Harry used to anger Diana greatly. The nonsense should be scotched here and now. Harry was born on 15 September, 1984. Diana did not meet James until the summer of 1986, and the red hair gossips so love to cite as proof is, of course, a Spencer trait.'

Even before Diana's death, Hewitt betrayed her. He collaborated with a book, *Princess in Love*, with the charming Anna Pasternak and pocketed a tidy sum. It was the first and most damning of his series of interviews and book deals, which left the affable officer branded a cad and disowned by his regiment. Hewitt had broken the golden rule and had spoken of his love affair. It is a 'crime' both Diana and Charles committed as well, but they seemed to escape the censure and outrage heaped on the unfortunate Major Hewitt.

But, since the death of the princess, that one question has dogged him – and Harry, too. Was he Harry's father? Yes they both had red hair, but, as we have seen, so did most of Harry's maternal family. In 2002 Hewitt did his best to dispel the rumours once and for all. In an interview with the tabloid *Sunday Mirror*, he said, 'There really is no possibility whatsoever that I am Harry's father. I can absolutely assure you that I am not. Admittedly, the red hair is similar to mine and people say we look alike. I have never encouraged these comparisons and although I was with Diana for a long time I must state once and for all that I'm not Harry's father. When I met Diana, he was already a toddler.'

With that the matter should have been closed. But there will always be those who make snide comments. Harry's close bond with his father is without doubt. Their love and mutual respect have gone a long way to shape Harry into the man he is today. Those close to Harry say that his attitude towards his detractors is to let them say what they want and forget about it.

Harry's army training continued after Sandhurst. He was sent on exercises and maintained himself at peak fitness. But the question on everybody's lips, including those of the prince himself, was, 'Will he get to serve in a conflict zone for real?' At first the military carefully sidestepped the issue; security matters are never discussed publicly and Harry's future deployment came under this category. But all the time there was stalemate on the deployment issue. Servicemen and -women were dying in Iraq and Afghanistan, some of whom had trained alongside the royal princes at Sandhurst. Could Harry seriously expect the top brass to send him into danger zones and risk the life of the Queen's grandson? Harry made it quite clear from the outset that he was deadly serious. He expected to do his duty and he would not be deterred due to his royal rank. He had trained as a soldier and that is exactly what he wanted to be.

Soon, stories began to circulate from sources close to the prince that, if he wasn't sent to Iraq with his regiment, he would quit the army. The official denials of these reports were lacklustre, too. The stories had the ring of truth. Everybody knew Harry would not be prepared to sit on his hands for long. It presented General Sir Richard Dannatt, Chief of the General Staff, with a real headache. There were those who thought it madness to send the prince to one of the most dangerous places on Earth where his very presence would put those serving alongside him at extra risk.

Others, rightly, thought it a waste of taxpayers' money to train Harry to be an officer in the British Army and then not allow him to use the expertise he had gleaned. Both had a point, and Sir Richard had a difficult tightrope to walk. Then, on 21 February 2007, came the announcement Harry had dreamed of. Ending weeks of speculation, the Ministry of Defence said Harry would be deployed with his Blues and Royals regiment in May or June that year. He would serve as a troop commander in charge of several light tank reconnaissance vehicles. The announcement meant that Harry would become the first royal to serve in a war zone since his uncle, Prince Andrew, the Duke of York, piloted helicopters in the Falklands conflict twenty-five years earlier.

The joint statement from the MoD and Clarence House read,

We can confirm today that Prince Harry will deploy to Iraq later this year in command of a troop from 'A Squadron' of the Household Cavalry Regiment. While in Iraq Cornet Wales will carry out a normal troop commander's role, involving leading a troop of 12 men in four Scimitar armoured reconnaissance vehicles, each with a crew of three. The decision to deploy him has been a military one ... The royal household has been consulted throughout.

The statement also warned of the hazards of press speculation on the exact location where he would serve, highlighting the security risks of the deployment. It was both dangerous and courageous at the same time. It was a personal triumph for Harry but at the same time he became the number-one target for insurgents. Personally, Harry was delighted by the news. He had always said he wanted to put his training into practice. At a farewell regimental party at a London nightclub, the prince admitted in a short speech that he was 'shitting himself'. After all he wasn't just any soldier.

Defence Minister Des Browne outlined that two squadrons from the Household Cavalry Regiment, of which Harry was part, were to be deployed. Ironically, the announcement came a day after Prime Minister Tony Blair had announced the phased withdrawal of British forces from the country, with the withdrawal of 1,600 troops within the coming months.

The reaction from the insurgents in Iraq was chilling. Abu Zaid, commander of the Mali Ibn Al Ashtar Brigade, was quoted as saying, 'We are awaiting the arrival of the young, handsome, spoiled prince with bated breath ... he will return to his grandmother but without ears.' Abu Samir, the leader of the Iranian-backed insurgent Sunni group Thar-allah (meaning God's revenge), said the soldier-prince could not avoid detection in southern Iraq. He also claimed that he had spies inside British bases who would notify insurgents immediately. Bluster? Perhaps, but it would have been foolish for General Dannatt to write off these bloodcurdling threats. There was very good reason to believe Harry would be specifically targeted.

What happened next was to test Harry to the limit. On 16 May 2007 General Dannatt announced that the prince would not be sent to Iraq after all because of the 'unacceptable risks'. The general was forced to intervene after receiving quality intelligence that a sniper, who had already killed six British troops in Basra, had been told that assassinating the prince was his priority. Another plot involved the scenario of Harry's being seized and smuggled across the border to Iran – where a rescue operation would have been all but impossible.

The army's intelligence machine backed up the claims. 'There have been a number of specific threats, some reported, and some not reported, which relate directly to Prince Harry as an individual,' General Dannatt explained. 'These threats expose not only him but also those around him to a degree of risk that I now deem unacceptable.'

The prince had suffered the highs and the lows of outrageous fortune within weeks. Within days of his expected deployment, his hopes had been dashed. Only time would tell whether these experiences would help him become a man.

General Dannatt said the prince had proved himself as an officer of 'determination and undoubted talent – and I do not say that lightly'.

Harry stayed out of the limelight. He was devastated by the news, and the blow was made more crushing by the fact that he had to bid farewell to his brother soldiers in his regiment as they went off to serve. Clarence House tried their best to play down Harry's devastation. A statement said he was 'very disappointed' but added that 'he fully understands and accepts General Dannatt's difficult decision and remains committed to his army career. Prince Harry's thoughts are with his troop and the rest of the battle group in Iraq.' Asked if Harry would quit the army as a result, a spokesman replied, 'Absolutely not.' But it was not a forgone conclusion by any stretch of the imagination.

The inevitable chorus of disapproval followed. Reg Keys – whose son Thomas had been killed while on active service in Basra in 2003 – said he found the decision 'distasteful' and questioned whether insurgents could have told the prince apart from other service personnel. 'It would appear that Harry's life is more valuable than my son or the other nearly 150 service personnel who've given their lives,' he added. It was just what the Queen, Harry and the army did not want to hear.

Republic, a group that campaigns for an elected head of state, had a field day. A spokesman said the decision showed that the prince should never have been allowed to join the army. 'This is a scandalous waste of taxpayer's money, brought on by the Windsor family's obsession with linking themselves to the military,' their statement said. Former Conservative Defence Secretary Michael Portillo also criticised the MoD for 'terrible vacillation' over the issue, and Tory MP Desmond Swayne – a former Territorial Army officer in Iraq – said the decision was a victory for Iraqi insurgents. Not for the first time Harry had become a political football.

Behind the scenes in the weeks leading up to the decision, Clarence House had written to all newspapers and broadcasters stating that reports about Harry's specific role in Iraq could cause serious risk to the lives of soldiers and civilians. They asked them not to report or speculate about the specific role Harry and his troop, his squadron or his regiment might have while on operation in Iraq; not to send reporters or photographers to cover Harry or his deployment without the express authorisation of the MoD press office; not to publish reports and photographs from unauthorised sources; and to check any story about Harry's deployment with the MoD. But the policy had failed. The continued press speculation about Harry's role in Iraq had made it almost impossible for him to serve.

Now the Royal Family's worst nightmare, that something dreadful might happen to Prince Harry in Iraq, had disappeared, to be replaced by one almost as terrifying. In this nightmare, there was a newspaper front page, some time in the future, bearing a picture of the prince staggering, bleary-eyed, out of a London nightclub. Also on the page was a news item, reporting casualties among the young British soldiers in Basra. Whatever happened next, observers claimed, the Harry-and-Iraq episode would rank high among Britain's great military cock-ups. How, columnists asked, did the Ministry of Defence, the army and Clarence House get it so wrong?

The answer, they said, lay in the appalling decision-making and lack of judgement that haunted the affair. It was mishandled from the very beginning and the bungling, some close to the Royal Family would say, went back to the death of Princess Diana. From that point onwards, the young princes had become accustomed to doing much as they pleased. Prince Philip argued long and hard against their joining the army. The Navy, in which Charles had served, was a more controlled environment, Philip said.

Diana's former private secretary, Patrick Jephson, a former Royal Navy commander, said, 'That is precisely why the Duke of Edinburgh was suggesting it. He is a pragmatist.'

The princes could have done their bit without being exposed to the special attentions of an enemy such as the Iranian-backed insurgents in Iraq. But, even as a child, Harry wanted to join the army. He insisted on military uniforms and combat gear for birthday presents and at the age of seven he borrowed a police radio from the security post at Kensington Palace, telling Diana's protection officer, Inspector Ken Wharfe, 'I have to get used to these radios because they have them in the army.' So, when the subject of military service was raised, his boyhood wish prevailed against the advice of his grandfather.

When Harry had graduated from Sandhurst the previous April, he chose to join the Household Cavalry regiment, the Blues and Royals. What seemed extraordinary was that nobody, with the exception of Prince Philip, had foreseen the looming problem. At that stage, Britain's forces were deeply engaged in highly dangerous operations in southern Iraq. The regiment Harry was joining specialised in medium reconnaissance, scouting out enemy-held terrain in light armour ahead of the main force.

In Iraq, the regiment conducts patrols that expose soldiers to insurgent sniper fire, ambushes and roadside bombs. Just weeks before the decision to ban Harry from the Iraqi frontline, insurgents blew up a Scimitar vehicle, killing two crewmen from the Queen's Royal Lancers. It was a clear signal for the MoD and General Dannatt. It was a situation that the army contemplated sending Harry into, leading a troop of eleven soldiers on some of the most dangerous missions of the conflict.

Rightly, the media began to question the common sense of Harry's army career. Why did no one see the impossible situation that it would create, not just for Harry but for those serving with him? It seemed incredible that the army had only just worked out he would become a special target. In fact, the truth is that they had known this for months, but a farcical game of politics and PR had been played behind the scenes. The army believed Harry was an asset and from his Sandhurst days used every opportunity to exploit his unique PR value. Pictures of the prince in combat gear were released, video footage of him on military exercises was made available and he even did a TV interview in which he talked about his army career and desire to see frontline action. Still, the warning signals were ignored. Then, as it became clear the Blues and Royals would be deployed in Basra, Clarence House and the MoD began showing signs of nervousness, even if Harry did not.

Prince Charles's director of communications, Paddy Harverson, and his then counterpart at the MoD, James Clark, both ex-journalists turned government PR men, issued a joint letter to newspaper editors in February 2007. It requested that restraint be exercised in stories relating to Harry. It said that his security could be compromised. A few weeks later, they wrote again, to say they were worried that their concerns were being overlooked. But editors were unwilling to allow the burden of Harry's security to be shifted onto them, especially since the PR people were suggesting there might be media access to Harry in the field. At that stage, with Harry now apparently heading for a war zone after all, numerous stories emerged. Clarence House and the MoD did not see fit to impose a blanket ban with a D-notice, a device that was used when Prince

Andrew served in the Falklands. Coverage of Harry's proposed role continued, without interference from the Royal Family or the military. Fortunately for Harry, the pair would have a chance to redeem themselves.

What followed was a series of shallow excuses. General Dannatt, an honourable and distinguished soldier, set about blaming news organisations for what was shaping up as a full-blown PR disaster. It seemed they had missed the fact that they had ignored a royal precedent on which it could have based its decisions. The Duke of Kent, who had a distinguished twenty-one-year career in the army, had been forbidden from serving in Northern Ireland during the civil conflict in the Seventies. It was thought the Queen's cousin would be a target for IRA terrorists. So why would Harry, a much more senior royal as third in line to the throne, be any different? He was now forced to sit and wait. He was not a quitter.

The final insult to the soldier-prince was served up by the American artist Daniel Edwards. He created a sculpture that featured Harry dead, laid out before the Union Flag with pennies placed over his eyes and his head resting on a bible, as he clutched a locket containing his mother's hair. It went on show at the Trafalgar Hotel in central London as part of the Bridge Art Fair. This work, said the New York-based artist, was intended to be seen as a memorial to honour those who are willing but unable to serve in Iraq.

'Prince Harry's spirit must have died the day they told him he couldn't serve,' he said. 'That's what this memorial is about.' The artwork was being amended to show the prince's head with his ears cut off, a reference to reports that militia leaders in Iraq had said they planned to send him back to his grandmother 'without his ears'.

Edwards said that a bronze casting of his 'severed ears' would go on display and go on sale on a website auction. An Art Fair spokesman, David Kesting, said, 'This war memorial is dedicated to the brave at heart. But the brave men and women Prince Harry inspired to enlist for combat following his announcement to serve six months in Iraq are not forgotten.'

It seemed more like a sick publicity stunt. Again, Harry kept a dignified silence. As far as he was concerned, his war was not over, so there was no need for statues.

CHAPTER ELEVEN
I'M NO QUITTER

*Courage is what it takes to stand up and speak; courage
is also what it takes to sit down and listen.'*
SIR WINSTON CHURCHILL

'I wouldn't use the word *quitting*,' Harry said as he tried to sidestep the delicate issue. 'It was a case of, "I very much feel like, if I'm going to cause this much chaos to a lot of people, then maybe I should bow out, and not just for my own sake, for everyone else's sake."'

The prince's admission that his leaving the army had been a real possibility showed just how seriously he took the decision that had been made not to deploy him to Iraq. If he had decided to leave his chosen career it would have been a huge disappointment not only to him personally but to the army and the palace, too. It would also have presented the palace mandarins with a very difficult problem: what to do next with Harry.

Many had seen a military career as the saving of the rebellious prince and had breathed a huge sigh of relief when he arrived at Sandhurst. For him to walk away so soon would have been a PR disaster on a par with his uncle

Prince Edward's decision to quit the Royal Marines twenty years earlier as a twenty-two-year-old during his one-year training tour.

Fortunately, wise heads prevailed. The Queen – as sovereign and ultimately Harry's commander-in-chief – and Prince Charles urged caution. Prince Philip, too, stressed the need for professional integrity, not only for himself but for the men and women serving in Iraq and Afghanistan. Harry had no choice but to sit tight and take the decision and the disappointment like a man and a soldier.

Those who predicted Harry would flounce out were to be disappointed. Harry knew the reasons for the U-turn and accepted them. 'I would never want to put someone else's life in danger when they have to sit next to the bullet magnet,' he explained. 'There was information that other people got that suggested that not only was my life in danger but the people that I served with. My being there may up the ante: rather than two contacts a day, it would be six or seven. That was a risk that they weren't willing to take, which I completely accepted.'

His first priority on hearing the news that he was to stay behind was to tell the soldiers who would have been under his command. He had just twenty minutes before the news broke on the media, and so he sat down with his men and, the best he could, talked through the reasons why his commanding officers had made the decision. The 'Toms' were baffled and felt somehow responsible for his disappointment. Harry explained, 'Before it got out in public I wanted to sit them down and say, "This is the story; this is what's happening; this is why" as much as I understood. They, being the soldiers that they are, said, "It's ridiculous. I would happily be under fire, be next to you as a troop leader" – all this sort of stuff, as any troop leader or any officer or soldier would expect from another soldier. It's a sort of brotherhood.'

Initially he had to join his brother William in D Squadron of the Blues and Royals, a holding unit destined never to go to war, made up of injured soldiers unfit to serve or those preparing to leave the regiment. His commanding officer assured him it was best to sit tight. The army, after all, was about finding solutions to problems. One would be found.

Soon, Harry was receiving reports from the guys in Iraq saying it really wasn't much fun. It was boiling hot and they were just sitting around, not actually being able to do anything. 'They were saying, "You're not missing out on anything; you're very lucky you're still back there."'

But Harry had no intention of just sitting on his hands and doing nothing. A face-to-face meeting between the prince and senior MoD figures, including General Dannatt, was organised in June. It was a crucial meeting that paved the way for him to embark on a tour to Afghanistan. Harry made it clear that he fully intended to serve as a frontline soldier and would do whatever was required to realise his ambition. He also stressed that he would consider leaving the army if a solution was not found. The top brass were determined not to lose him and hatched a plan for him to retrain as a battlefield air controller. It was enough to stop Harry bowing out. It mattered hugely to the ministry that they get their man onto the frontline.

General Dannatt then met with military commanders and told them it was imperative that a workable solution be found. One possibility discussed was a deployment with a United Nations force, which would enable him to serve in trouble spots in Africa or Bosnia, where the risk of being directly targeted by insurgents was considerably less. But many, including Harry, feared this would be seen as a cop-out.

The General knew that, before it could happen, the media had to be in on the secret. It went against the grain, but he had to trust them. In September, he held the first of a series of meetings with twenty-five senior executives from the main press and broadcasting organisations. They included Fleet Street editors, many of whom had published detailed reports about Harry's on/off deployment to Iraq. But this was no time for finger-pointing. If Harry was going to go to war, Dannatt said, there would have to be a news blackout and he could achieve that only with the full cooperation of the media. He was determined that, if an opportunity arose to deploy the prince again, there should not be a repeat of the previous fiasco.

The meetings, also attended by Prince Charles's press spokesman, Paddy Harverson, who sat silently at the back of the room, allowing the general and his communications team to take the lead, were strictly off the record. Senior Fleet Street figures, including editors from national newspapers, attended on the condition that nothing appeared in print. One source told me later, 'We were left in no doubt that the general felt backed into a corner. He was effectively saying that he had no choice but to get the young man into a conflict zone whatever it took. If he was there just for a day and had to be pulled out it didn't seem to matter. They genuinely didn't know if a news blackout during the prince's deployment was workable.'

Some of the media people were dubious whether a news blackout could hold, and rightly argued that, in return for their combined silence, they would require access to Harry before, during and after his tour of duty so the story could be told once the news of his deployment broke. They drew parallels with the way that newspapers, at the request of the police, have kept quiet about kidnappings in return for being given the full story at the end, once the danger has passed. It was a good call. General Dannatt could see the logic. A deal was struck, but as the British media executive argued, they could not be held responsible for the foreign media and the Internet.

Fortunately, for the top brass at least, the tenth anniversary of his mother's death provided a distraction for the prince. He and William decided, as the controversy over the *manner* of Diana's death raged, that they should take charge of her legacy. While others, notably Mohamed al-Fayed, the father of Diana's last lover Dodi, who died alongside her, peddled conspiracy theories that would ultimately be dismissed by an inquest jury in 2008, the princess's sons wanted their mother to be remembered for the good she achieved in her life. They decided on a two-pronged memorial.

First, they organised a charity pop concert starring Elton John, Joss Stone, Rod Stewart, Duran Duran and Lily Allen in her memory at the new £800 million Wembley Stadium to be held on what would have been her forty-sixth birthday. It was followed by a service of thanksgiving. They also agreed to a series of interviews in which they would talk openly about her. During a walkabout ahead of the concert, William joked that his brother was 'the ginger Bob Geldof' – a reference to the organiser of the Live Aid concert staged at the old Wembley Stadium and attended by their late mother more than twenty years before. And

Harry admitted in an interview with the BBC's Fearne Cotton, 'If it goes wrong it'll be very nerve-racking.'

He promised an amazing evening and he delivered. But, even as he prepared to party with the stars and his girlfriend Chelsy, his thoughts were with his regiment and the men serving in Iraq. He and William addressed a crowd of 63,000 inside the stadium and a global television audience of 500 million watching in 140 different countries. Harry knew he had a captive audience and chose the moment to send a clear message to his brother soldiers and to his commanding officer. 'I wish I was there with you. I'm sorry I can't be. But, to all of those on operations at the moment, we'd both like to say: stay safe.'

The frustration soon set in and, once again, Harry was on the front pages for the wrong reasons. There were reports that the prince was 'depressed' and wanted to quit the army early. A few weeks later, in June, he flew to the British Army Training Unit in Suffield in Alberta, Canada, for exercises using live ammunition. It was the largest area available for British armoured vehicles to practise fire-and-manoeuvre operations. It was supposed to be a way of keeping the prince out of the limelight. The opposite happened. He was left with some explaining to do when he was photographed in drunken clinches with provocatively dressed barmaids at Calgary's Cowboys bar while enjoying off-duty downtime. Harry was reported to have asked one whether she was wearing any underwear and declared, 'I want to see all the beautiful girls.'

Cherie Cymbalisty, aged twenty-two, recognised him immediately despite his attempts to go undercover by claiming his name was Gary. 'He was very forward and told me I was stunning. He was really interested in my tattoos and wanted to see them more closely,' she said. Wearing a T-shirt and cap, he spent the evening drinking beer, sambuca shots and rum and Coke and posing for photographs with Miss Cymbalisty and her friends. 'He leaned in to kiss me on both cheeks and then on the lips. He certainly didn't mention anything about having a girlfriend. He sure didn't act like he had one,' the barmaid claimed.

Harry then asked for her mobile number and sent a text message arranging to come back when the bar closed. She declined an offer to carry on 'partying' at their barracks and apparently received a text message from the prince the next morning. It reportedly said,

What happened to u last night babe. U disappeared. We waited for u outside coz apparently u were keen to come back to party?! Loser, guess u didn't have the stamina, hey?!!! We went all night and u were v missed! X

The unedifying episode exasperated many of his father's aides back home. While defending Harry's right to enjoy a night out, one official expressed incredulity at the prince's 'lack of foresight' in allowing himself to be photographed in such a compromising position while the rest of his regiment was fighting in Iraq. 'He's not a bad lad by any stretch of the imagination, but his antics show an unforgivable lack of common sense.' As the story broke, a member of the First Battalion of the Grenadier Guards became the sixtieth British soldier to be killed in Afghanistan since 2001. Guardsman Neil 'Tony' Downes, a twenty-year-old from Manchester, was in a Land Rover on patrol with the Afghan National Army close to the town of Sangin in Helmand Province when the vehicle was hit by a roadside bomb. The contrast could not have been starker.

When Harry returned to the UK there were more *faux pas*. During a trip to the Royal Navy's fleet diving squadron in Portsmouth, in his role as Commodore-in-Chief of Small Ships and Diving, he had a light-hearted run-in with the press who went there to photograph him. As he appeared before the media in a wet suit with the word 'Wales' on his head gear, he joked, 'You bastards!' Paddy Harverson subsequently insisted that the outburst be not reported. Bizarrely, the PR man's 'instruction' stuck.

It was not so easy to gag Harry's girlfriend. She was still smarting from the reports of her boyfriend's behaviour in the Canadian bar. He had tried to dismiss it as just boys' night out, but the Zimbabwean-born heiress was growing tired of Harry's excuses. She felt let down. She had been there for him when he needed her. 'She helped him deal with the Iraq thing and this is how he repaid her,' said a close source. 'She felt really badly let down and told him so.'

The prince had enjoyed a passionate three-year relationship with Chelsy. It had been volatile, both storming out on each other. But they had always been reconciled. He had fallen for Chelsy within four days of meeting her and poured out his heart about her to fellow travellers at a campfire beside Botswana's Okavango River. They had always been open about their love. At the Wembley concert for Diana, they had sat in the front of the Royal Box openly kissing and hugging, not caring who was watching, while his brother William and girlfriend Kate sat apart, despite the fact that they had rekindled their romance.

But now the Stowe-educated postgraduate was growing

tired of being humiliated by a seemingly endless parade of photographs and lurid stories about Harry's wandering eye. She threatened to end their relationship, forcing him to beg her to reconsider. He promised to make it up to her on a make-or-break holiday in Botswana. They agreed to patch it up, but Chelsy's trust appeared to be waning. She had already accepted a place at Leeds University for a postgraduate law degree and was coming to Britain anyway. She would give him another chance.

Within weeks, racked by homesickness at Leeds and feeling increasingly isolated as Harry was away on military training commitments, Chelsy decided to end their relationship. Friends explained that she had simply fallen out of love with the prince. The last straw was him missing her twenty-second birthday for the rugby World Cup final in Paris. A senior palace official told the *News of the World*, the paper that broke the story, 'The relationship is over. It has simply run its course.'

The end finally came in a series of long-distance phone calls while Harry was doing charity work in Lesotho and Chelsy was at her student digs in Leeds. She was, apparently, fed up with the fact that Harry was not putting the maximum amount of effort into the relationship. Soon, his maximum efforts would have to be diverted to his career. In secret, he had been undergoing intensive retraining as a battlefield air controller known as a JTAC (joint terminal attack controller) with a view to going to Afghanistan. There could no guarantees but the prince had to be prepared.

Within weeks of his split from Chelsy, Harry's long wait was finally over. As a grandmother, the Queen had shared Harry's frustration over Iraq. As his sovereign and commander-in-chief she took it upon herself personally to give him the news he was desperate to hear. If she had mixed emotions about his going to one of the most dangerous places on Earth, she didn't show it when she broke the news. Asked whether he had told his grandmother of the final decision to send him, he revealed, 'She actually told me. She told me I'm off to Afghanistan, so that was the way it was supposed to be.'

The Queen, ever the pragmatist, had always been a strong supporter of his desire to serve on the frontline, despite his royal rank. Now she was 'relieved' that he could finally do the job he had trained so hard for. She had witnessed at first hand Harry's frustration over his failure to be deployed to Iraq. 'She and everybody else did,' the prince admitted. 'There was a lot of frustration but, as they say in the army, "Turn to the right and carry on."'

This time, only a close circle of family, friends and as few as fifteen Ministry of Defence senior officials were told in advance. They knew any leaks would make the prince and those around him more of a target. From the outset the Queen had asked General Dannatt to keep her informed of the situation. The two had discussed the situation. 'We've had a lot of talks about it since April, the last time it was supposed to happen.' Harry said. 'She was very "pro" my going then, so I think she's relieved that I get the chance to do what I want to do. She's a very good person to talk to about it. Her knowledge of the army is amazing for a grandmother – I suppose it's slightly her job.'

He was elated. He had one last task to fulfil before he could say his final goodbyes. He slipped into Clarence House in civilian clothes for a top-secret media interview, part of the deal with the press in exchange for their silence.

Above: Prince Harry studies a map.

Below: Cleaning the dust from the machine gun on his Spartan.

For personal protection Prince Harry carried a 9mm pistol and body armour in the desert.

Above: Harry takes a picture of the sunset.

Below: Talking to a local Afghan man, Harry shows him the route around a British Army cordon.

Above: Prince Harry steps off a military transport plane shortly after landing at RAF Brize Norton as he returns from his 10 weeks' curtailed tour of duty in Afghanistan.

Below: Leaving the departures terminal at RAF Brize Norton with his father, the Prince of Wales, and his brother Prince William.

Harry talks of his recent tour of duty during a TV interview held after his arrival back in the UK in early March 2008.

Harry and his girlfriend Chelsy Davy leave the Army garrison church in Windsor after a service of remembrance for the casualties of Afghanistan.

Above: Harry marches through the streets of Windsor with fellow soldiers of the British Army.

Below: His aunt, Princess Anne, awards Harry his campaign service medal.

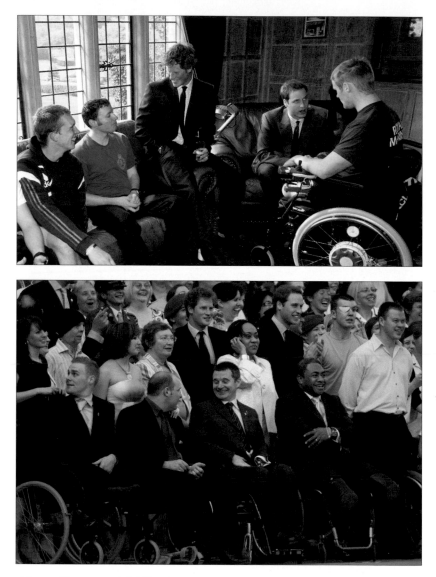

Above: Harry and William speak with servicemen injured in the course of duties in Afghanistan, at Headley Court Rehabilitation Centre, Epsom, in April 2008.

Below: The princes attend the City Salute sunset pageant in London in May 2008. The event was held to thank British troops and their families for the sacrifices they make on their nation's behalf – true heroes, every one of them.

Only a handful of people knew about his deployment and Clarence House were taking no chances.

Harry's relationship with the media had not always been cordial. His mother's death and the involvement on the paparazzi clouded it. But he was a soldier now as well as a prince, and the interview was just part of the job. It was straightforward stuff. The questions had been cleared beforehand. There would be nothing the handpicked journalists would ask to catch him out, but he was careful just the same.

What was his reaction when he heard he would be going? one asked. He had had a few minutes to prepare and knew exactly what he would say. 'A bit of excitement, a bit of, "Phew! Finally get the chance to actually do the soldiering I wanted to do from ever since I joined,"' he replied. He was 'still slightly unclear' about what he would be doing precisely, but everyone going on operations in Afghanistan would have to get used to multitasking, he said. 'You've got one job that you go out there for,' he said, 'but when you actually get out there you're being pulled left, right and centre helping out people.'

Essentially, he explained, he was going to be with TACP, which is Tactical Air Control Party, linked in with the RAF and fast jets and supply drops. A kind of air-traffic controller, a somewhat different role I never thought I would see myself doing in the army.

'I have been trained for it. I haven't spent a day at Heathrow or anything like that, but, to the extent that the army can train you for air-traffic controlling, I have been trained for it. It's very different from reconnaissance work, "eyes and ears".'

Rather than troop leader, the eyes and ears in a

different area, his new role would be on a 'bigger scale', He joked, 'I'll be with the higher-up people, hopefully trying to advise them on how to use air, but I'm sure they won't take my advice.' He laughed. It was apparent he was still unclear of exactly what he would be doing when he got to Afghanistan. He would soon find that out in the theatre of war.

Harry's deployment had been shrouded in secrecy. It had all been on a need-to-know basis. Even some senior officials at Clarence House, his father's private office, did not know. Most of his close friends had to be kept out of the loop, too. 'It was a decision of mine and other people to basically keep it as quiet as possible for the obvious reasons, as last time it was slightly ruined but this time it seems as though it has all been good.'

He had told a few people. His on/off girlfriend Chelsy knew and of course his immediate family, but that was about it. 'I have told the people that I feel would need to know but other people I don't really want to put in that position of saying, "Right, I'm going," and then they feel as though they've got to keep that deep down inside. People will be nervous, I think, for me,' he explained.

'I hope and it will be a bit of a shock or surprise when they find out that I'm actually out there,' he said. Of course it would be.

Those who thought his tour of duty would be risk-free were in dreamland. Although the MoD had taken every precaution, there was no way any soldier, even a prince, could be guaranteed safety. 'No, it won't be risk-free,' Harry said, 'but, then, I didn't join the army thinking that I was never going to go on operations. Nowadays, especially in the world that we live in, it has got to that situation where people join the army to almost go on operations and to serve their country, to help in the little way that they can.'

He had never been to Afghanistan. It was no great holiday resort, he joked. 'It's winter, which is a slight disappointment. It's just going to be a little bit cold, a bit snowy, but at least we might have a white Christmas.'

Harry tried to keep the interview light-hearted. It was smattered with laughter and jokes. But he knew war was a serious business. With war came bloodshed, tears and death, and he was aware of that. When asked if he had known people who had died or were injured in Iraq and Afghanistan, his demeanour changed. He paused and reflected before answering.

'Mainly, well not mainly, but yes, injured. William and I were down at Headley Court the other day just meeting all the people that actually don't get recognition, all the guys who lost their limbs in one way or another. There's one, two, people that I knew of who died out there – they weren't, sort of, close to me but at the end of the day they wear the same uniform as you, they are brothers or close mates, so, yes, it does happen.

'And if that is spending six months in the army and then your second six months in Afghanistan and then for the soldier to sign off after that, well I don't see any problem with that at all. They have served their country in the little way that they can. And now that soldiers go on operations for six months they get back and they think, "Well, I've done my bit. How much more can be asked of me?" So without getting political...'

Politics, he knew as a royal, is a no-go zone. But even before he went into action he was thinking of his injured comrades. In his interview he called for more to be done for injured servicemen and -women and publicly backed the Help for Heroes charity, a cause this book is supporting by donating a proportion of any profits. It is a subject he, and his brother William, passionately support.

He went on, 'The Help for Heroes charity that's being set up at the moment by numerous people just brings awareness of the other casualties that are slightly, sort of, skipped over from coming back from operations. There's a lot that happens that the British public don't know about. It's a shame to see stories about Afghanistan and Iraq being pushed back to Page Six or Seven in the newspapers – they are our boys and they should be on the front page.' Soon, with Harry's involvement, it would soon be front-page news around the world.

Was he cut out for the job, a born leader? Harry was asked. 'Some people say I am. I enjoy it. I enjoy looking after people, not necessarily taking the reins and leading people, but I enjoy guys coming up to me to ask me for my opinion or help or whatever in that sense of the word and getting on and getting the job done with a bunch of really good guys.'

Within days he would put those leadership skills to the test. On 14 December, the prince secretly slipped out of the country on a troop flight bound for Kandahar, Afghanistan. He was destined for Garmsir in the far south of lawless Helmand Province, operating just 500 metres from frontline Taliban positions. It was lawless country at the heart of Afghanistan's opium trade, one of the most dangerous places in Earth.

Harry's war was about to begin for real.

CHAPTER TWELVE

WIDOW SIX SEVEN

When you're wounded and left on Afghanistan's plains,
And the women come out to cut up what remains,
Just roll to your rifle and blow out your brains
An' go to your Gawd like a soldier.
RUDYARD KIPLING, 'THE YOUNG BRITISH SOLDIER'

Defence Secretary John Reid got to his feet in the House of Commons. Despite his grave expression, he looked less self-assured than usual as he prepared to make his statement. The House was hushed. The MPs on all sides knew that the usual knockabout banter would have been inappropriate. Reid was fully aware that what he was about to say would, when translated into action, be measured in the number of brave men and women who would lose their lives and leave their families devastated for ever.

It was 26 January 2006. Britain was already heavily committed in Iraq. Now, he announced, our troops were to be sent to Helmand Province in the spring. It would be 'more demanding' than other regions of Afghanistan. Our troops would be a 'potent force' against the Taliban and drugs barons. An extra 3,300 troops would join the 1,100 already in theatre. The total could rise to a maximum of

5,700 but no more. He made no apology for the deployment, which would cost £1billion over three years.

'What matters is that we put the right forces in to do the job and to do it safely and to do it well,' he said.

The mission would need many more servicemen and women than at first thought. This was not a counterterrorism mission but a real effort to stop the country falling back into the clutches of the Taliban. 'We will not allow that and the Afghan people will not allow that,' he pronounced in his Lanarkshire twang. This was another emergency.

Those who knew their military history were pessimistic. They had every right to be. The British had come unstuck there before during the First and Second Afghan Wars. Some cited the disasters such as the retreat from Kabul as long ago as 1842. Of the 16,500 soldiers who set off, only a handful made it back to camp in Jalalabad alive. The rest had been killed by relentless attacks by tribesmen or the freezing weather.

Perhaps more relevant was the failure of the Soviet Union in the same mountainous country more than a century later. Even the might of the Red Army was unable to smash the spirit of the tribal peoples of Afghanistan. The Pashtuns, Durrani and Ghilzai may have found it impossible to live together; bloody feuds lasting generations were still commonplace. But they were passionately united in their hatred of intruders who invaded their country.

The Mujahideen resistance had been fierce, and in February 1989 – a decade after the Soviet Fortieth Army invasion force had rolled across the border to support the Marxist government – the final troops withdrew. It had been, some said, the Soviets' own Vietnam.

The world changed for ever after 9/11. In 2001 the British had been under pressure from their American allies to supply troops to back the ongoing NATO mission of trying to keep Afghanistan stable. By now, the easy parts had been done. The country had a democratically elected leader, President Hamid Karzai, and areas around Kabul in the northern and western regions were relatively peaceful. Now the Americans wanted Tony Blair to help them focus on the lawless southern regions, to smash the Taliban once and for all.

It was a desperate place that had been largely neglected. In 2002 the Americans had focused their efforts on destroying the Taliban in the mountainous east of the country. Aid that had been promised had been slow in reaching the south. So, in the absence of foreign troops, many of the Taliban fighters who had fled across the border to Pakistan after their defeat had drifted back to Kandahar, the birthplace of their extremist Islamic movement, and into Helmand Province itself. By 2006, when Dr Reid committed the troops, the Taliban had been busy re-establishing themselves through violence and intimidation and murder of sympathisers of NATO and the Karzai government.

Combating the Taliban resurgence was the battle group's main task. But there was a further aspect to the mission. Then, said Reid, troops would be expected to 'support international efforts to counter the narcotics trade, which poisons the economy of Afghanistan', He claimed that 90 per cent of the heroin on British streets originated there. Was he for real? It was a noble cause but not all the troops saw it his way. They knew this was not a risk-free exercise in building a nation. There would be hand-to-hand fighting with a tough and dedicated enemy who believed God was on their side.

During a barely audible satellite-phone interview from Kandahar during an official visit for Radio 4's *Today* programme, he bizarrely stated, 'if we came for three years here to accomplish our mission and had not fired one shot at the end of it we would be very happy indeed.' But what were the chances of that? Was he in cloud cuckoo land? Certainly many of the soldiers bound for the region thought so.

A website popular with soldiers – Army Rumour Service – highlighted some unease. One user had a specific message for Reid:

> If I have to bull [polish] my boots and carry any mates off the back of a[n RAF] hercules Mr Reid needs to know that I will hold him personally responsible. If it's me being carried then I will have left explicit instructions and half of my life insurance to someone who will avenge me.

And his idea that their presence would allow aid workers to help opium growers develop alternative sources of income did not fare much better. 'Wouldn't it be a damn sight easier and cheaper just to buy up the opium stocks?' another wrote. While another asked, 'How much of the heroin on the streets of Marseilles, Lyons and Paris ALSO originates in Afghanistan and are France going to participate in this NATO op?'

Perhaps as a well-read and passionate historian, Dr Reid should have picked up a copy of Rudyard Kipling's *Barrack-Room Ballads*, published in 1892. A century or so earlier, his predecessor would most certainly have done so.

They contained a poem called 'The Young British Soldier', much quoted at the time by those predicting disastrous consequences for anyone getting mixed up in Afghanistan. Had anything really changed since Kipling's day? One twenty-three-year-old redheaded soldier, who also happened to be third in line to the British throne, was about to find out. On 14 December, Harry had left RAF Brize Norton in Oxfordshire aboard the massive C-17 transport carrier aircraft. The previous day he had packed his Bergen rucksack. Every pouch was stuffed to bursting. His SA80A2 rifle and 9mm pistol were travelling separately under guard, but there was still his Osprey body armour, Kevlar helmet, rucksack, radio, doss bag, air bed, goggles as well as his sun cream. The list had stretched to a hundred lines. Finally everything was packed. He was good to go.

He had got his head down among the plane's cavernous hold during the twelve-hour journey. He and the other soldiers had dossed down on sleeping bags between the loads. The lights dimmed and the prince donned his helmet and body armour in case of a real risk of ground attack on landing. On the ground, lounging on battered chairs in a dusty operations room, Harry had listened to the arrival briefing spelling out the tactical situation in Afghanistan. He was told where to eat and sleep, the essentials for any soldier, as well as the imminent threat to the Coalition forces.

With all the information ringing in his head he crashed out on a camp bed. The first two days were going to be intense and he knew sleep was imperative. During the next forty-eight hours he would be given a crash course in the latest infantry techniques – an 'in-theatre training package'.

At the end of it he would be in no doubt what would be expected of him. He had donned a special SAS smock that had been given to him, while others wore the standard-issue desert-coloured ones. He had customised the front of his body armour, too, proudly displaying an Estonian army badge depicting an eagle, a personal souvenir.

Then, after being issued with live ammunition and morphine, worn around the neck with his ID tags in case of injury, Harry had a hairy flight south in a Chinook helicopter on 16 December. It was carrying Special Forces, and Harry hitched a ride. At last he was going closer to the action. His destination was FOB Dwyer, an isolated outpost in the middle of Helmand Province, southern Afghanistan.

Chillingly, the base was named after a young soldier of Harry's age who had been killed by a landmine the previous year. Ringed by a ditch and razor wire and with walls built from 5-foot-high wire-reinforced fabric containers of sand and gravel, it was heavily protected. The perimeter was protected by a devastating array of weaponry, including heavy machine guns. It was just 7 miles from the deserted frontline town of Garmsir, a major crossing point on the Helmand River and a 'choke point' for Taliban forces and equipment coming across the Pakistan border.

Harry was shattered. His exhaustion could not hide his elation. He had made it to the frontline. He was not there just to look pretty. He had trained hard and he had a real job to do.

To the fighter pilots and the crews manning spy planes above the battlefields of Afghanistan he was just Widow Six Seven, another radio call sign, a reassuring voice of authority, a brother in arms, a bit of a wag and, in Harry's case, an incorrigible flirt. It seemed you could take the boy out of Boujis, his favourite London nightclub, but not take Boujis out of the boy.

Laughter could be heard coming from the control. Much to the amusement of his colleagues, Harry chatted with a female Harrier pilot, Michelle Tompkins about the snow-covered mountains over which she was soaring and commented on how perfect they would be for a spot of skiing. Moments later, a separate radio channel crackled into life with Harry's laughing comrades telling him to 'get a room' if he was planning on pursuing that line of chat.

Harry's commanding officer, Battery Commander Major Andy Dimmock, saw the funny side: 'We were obviously giving him the mickey. We said, "Flirt with her any longer and you have to get a room." He said, "Does that count as the Mile-High Club?" For Harry, and for his fellow soldiers, such joking asides were a welcome relief amid work that could be both tense and tiresome.

Miles from home and with only sporadic communication with loved ones, banter and camaraderie were what passed as normality. They became a vital release amid the terrible business of war that would otherwise be too grim and too brutal to contemplate fully. Harry and his comrades were happy to share in the good-natured humour that punctuated the tedium of long hours scrutinising surveillance footage from the spy planes at work over southern Afghanistan.

During one long day shift, after Harry had spent hours communicating with one particular crew on a Nimrod spy plane, the aircraft's pilot turned the onboard camera around to flash a picture of a topless glamour model, taped to the outside of the surveillance craft, down to the control room below. After all, a war wouldn't be a war without a pin-up or two, and for the Facebook generation, of which Harry and his comrades were a part, the days of saucy playing cards viewed by torchlight had been replaced by live video feed and Internet downloads – although later in his tour, during downtime, Harry was photographed flicking through the lads' magazine *Zoo*, admiring models Emma Frain and Amli Grove. Back home the glamour models seemed pleased that her curves met with royal approval. 'I'm really flattered,' the twenty-year-old said.

Harry smiled to himself. He knew the pilot would see the funny side when his anonymity was blown. He noted, 'If he hasn't worked out [who I am], I'm sure when he sees this he'll wet himself – especially after that poster he showed me from several thousand feet.' On another occasion, while watching the dark figure of a Taliban fighter on his screen, Harry could be heard discussing the chances of his disappearing into a bunker. The pilot jokingly placed a bet of £10,000, to which Harry responded, 'I'll raise you half a million.'

'You couldn't afford it,' came the pilot's reply, not knowing that the voice on the other end was of a young man with a trust fund worth millions and whose grandmother was one of the richest women in the world.

A well as British and American pilots, the prince's job also brought him into communication with French and Dutch jets. Harry could manage only a few French phrases, but he said, 'They're quite entertaining and amusing. It's always funny because it's almost as though their nose is being pinched because of the air oxygen [mask]. It's like something out of *Monty Python*.'

While he was stripped of the anonymity he so enjoyed during his tour of duty, the banter, especially when no one else could listen to it, was an essential part of the job. 'It's just me and him [the pilot] having a good banter and obviously when the aircraft come in you know you've got them on task for three, three and a half hours and you're looking for possibly one or two enemy digging a trench and it can get quite tiring. If you're just saying, "Yep, go to this point" and just putting the radio down and staring at the screen, it just sends you insane. So I think it's good to be relaxed on the net and have a good chat, but when things are pretty hairy then you need to obviously turn on your game face and do the job.'

Harry's light-hearted account of his role belied the truth. In the ops room an array of sophisticated reconnaissance equipment provided a live videofeed on to a laptop computer. Harry and his pals dubbed it 'Taliban TV' or 'Kill TV'. Explaining his role Harry told an interviewer: 'Terry Taliban and his mates, as soon as they hear air [jets], they go to ground, which makes life a little bit tricky.' But the hi-tech visual feedback meant Harry could follow them.

It was a baptism of fire for the second lieutenant. He needed a crash course and, luckily, he found the right guy for the job, Corporal David Baxter, a veteran of nine years' service completing tours in Iraq and Kosovo as well as Afghanistan. Baxter, aged twenty-eight, was only two months into his tour of duty when he found himself mentoring Prince Harry, one of his regiment's youngest officers. The former tank driver from Bendooragh near Coleraine in Northern Ireland, an NCO in the Lifeguards, was sent to Helmand in the autumn to work, like Harry, as a forward air controller. Initially, he was part of a two-man team working with a South African captain. But when, having done consecutive tours in Iraq and Afghanistan without a well-earned break, his work partner went home on leave to be replaced by the newly trained prince, the two men hit it off immediately.

'He's a really down-to-earth person,' Baxter said. 'To be honest, I don't think anyone thinks of him as third in line to the throne or anything. You just take him at face value as any other officer.'

The two had not previously been close friends but David had been used to seeing Harry around, as they are both part of the Household Cavalry. 'His arrival, as far as I could tell, was kept quite hush-hush. A lot of people didn't know he was coming out but he's fitted in really well. Everyone from the Household Cavalry Regiment knows him, has worked with him for about a year or so now.

'We're used to having him about, so it's not really been any change for us ... it has just been a surprise for those that are attached, such as the gunners. They were initially surprised to see him ... but at the end of the day he's just treated the same as any other officer from the regiment,' he said.

Widow Six Seven impressed the corporal. 'The first time he took over the net from his predecessor he was straight in there,' he explained. 'He's really confident and sounded like he'd been there for quite a considerable amount of time. He's always got a rapport with the pilots that he's talking to. I'm sure they would be quite shocked as well if they knew who they were talking to,' he said.

During the long shifts in the battle group operations room, it was not long before the two red-heads were sharing jokes and laddish banter. Harry recalled, 'He fixed my radio for me so he's a good guy to have on board, despite being ginger and Irish. It's a lethal mix.'

It was obvious to David that Harry was delighted just to be there. 'I think a lot of people are more happy for him. He was quite disappointed with the fact that he couldn't get out to Iraq. For any soldier to be told that they can't go on tour for whatever reason is quite disappointing and most people are actually just glad to see that he has been able to do the job that he trained to do,' he said.

But it was not all about banter and backslapping for making it to the war zone. As an emergency air controller he had played a real role in the war. He had helped rescue under-fire comrades by calling in bomber jets. Soon he would get a taste of real action. One senior officer emphasised the point: 'As a professional soldier, Harry is trained to kill the enemy – that is his job. He is no different to anyone else in uniform.'

As his close family were arriving for the traditional festive celebrations at Sandringham, the Queen's estate in Norfolk, Harry prepared to join the Gurkhas at FOB Delhi in downtown Garmsir. The Prince of Wales, like any parent of a serviceman, was worried for his safety. He was putting on a brave face. It was, after all, his duty, and the royals were all about duty. The Queen and the rest of the royals raised their glasses to the soldier-prince. She had been there before, when her second son Andrew had served in the Falklands. Privately, they all prayed for his safe return. The media for once were as good as their word. They kept to their end of a bargain that, in an age of twenty-four-hour news, was no mean feat. Reports said that both princes could not join their eighty-one-year-old grandmother because they were on regimental duties over the Christmas period.

The Queen's speech – made available on the Internet for the first time, via the Royal Family's video channel on YouTube – was particularly poignant for her family. As footage of the Royal Marines in Afghanistan was shown, she said, 'I want to draw attention to another group of people who deserve our thoughts this Christmas. We have all been conscious of those who have given their lives, or who have been severely wounded, while serving with the Armed Forces in Iraq and Afghanistan.'

Her audience remained blissfully unaware that her own grandson was among their throng. The day before Harry had arrived at FOB Delhi, he had been ordered forward to join the Gurkhas. The town's high street was the British frontline, the start of a 500-metre no-man's-land of bombed trenches, irrigation ditches and shattered farms. If anyone had doubted his commitment to be a frontline soldier, they had been proved wrong.

CHAPTER THIRTEEN

FRONTLINE SOLDIER

Yes; quaint and curious war is!
You shoot a fellow down
You'd treat if met where any bar is,
Or help to half-a-crown.
THOMAS HARDY, FROM THE POEM: 'THE MAN HE KILLED'

Harry Wales didn't attract a second glance as he patrolled the bombed-out streets of Garmsir. Why would he? After all, he was just another British solider, anonymous in battle fatigues. Most of the women and children had long gone. A young boy, one of the few who had drifted back, passed him by riding a donkey, his feet nearly touching the ground. The place was evocative of a scene from an old Wild West movie – one showing the exhausted aftermath of a bloody gunfight in a dusty border town.

Everywhere there were signs that this ghost town was once a thriving centre. Smashed television sets spilled out from the front of a group of shops that were once busy electrical stores. Odd trainers were scattered across the dusty main street, from what was once a shoe shop at the corner. Afghan bank notes, blown around by the dusty breeze, were strewn everywhere. In the searing heat of the day, only a few bearded men remained, relaxing in the cooler shade of shattered buildings, their rifles never far away.

The walls of Harry's new 'home' bore testament to the men who had passed through the gates of the base before him: the names of those who have served and survived. They had 'lived the dream', as the soldiers put it, inscribed for posterity. Next to them there were tributes to the less fortunate souls, the brave men who never went home – heartfelt memorials, painted by their pals.

Harry was under no illusion that he was now at the sharp end of Afghanistan's frontline. His tiny, Spartan camp, had, along with the nearby eastern checkpoint, been repeatedly attacked by the Taliban since the British moved in 2006. At least he could be grateful that his sleeping billet was mortar-proof. It had to be. Taliban rockets and rocket-propelled grenades (RPGs) had got through, causing devastating injuries. It was a harsh environment – a collection of bomb-ravaged buildings, shipping containers and army hardware with fortifications and observation posts at every turn. There were two rectangular mud-walled compounds with watchtowers on the corners. Over the months, the men had added personal touches: family photographs, children's drawings, pictures of half-naked women ripped from magazines and football flags proclaiming loyalty to different teams were scattered around.

His new home had once been a US agricultural college, but its new incarnation could not be further removed. It had changed hands several times and was once even a Taliban madrassa (an Islamic school). The camp, a series of connected observation positions, came under attack several times a day with RPGs, mortar shells and machine-gun fire. Major Mark Milford, of the First Battalion of the Royal

Gurkha Rifles, Harry's direct boss at the camp, was asked whether this was a safe place for a prince. 'No, not really,' he replied in a matter-of-fact manner. How could it be?

Sand, like talcum powder, at times ankle-deep, covered every arid inch, throwing up a dust film that managed to permeate the smallest crevice. Even the most airtight containers for some reason could not escape the dust. By day, the furnace-like temperatures meant that the men's thirst was constant. But the bottled water, airlifted in like everything else, was strictly rationed.

The soldier-prince was quick on the uptake. He soon learned one top tip: old socks dampened and placed round the water bottle kept his water cool. As the liquid evaporated, the water inside the bottle was cooled. After their one bottle a day had been consumed, the men had to be content with the foul-tasting chlorinated water, made more palatable by adding flavoured powder or 'screech' as they call it. Washing facilities were even more restricted. Harry and his comrades could only dream of the luxuries such as a tiled bathroom, let alone a royal palace previously enjoyed by Second Lieutenant Wales.

At Dwyer no one was allowed to wash before 11 a.m., because what little running water was available was still frozen due to the freezing temperatures at night. At Delhi there was no running water. The 'showers' were simply a bag hung up in an outdoor wooden cubicle. Instead, Harry had to make do with lugging jerry cans of water for his ablutions. Carefully limited amounts are poured into washing bowls or a couple of solar showers surrounded by basic wooden shelters. Shaving had to be restricted to once every three days. The rounded ends of missile cases made do as shaving bowls. Some hot water was available from a

'Puffing Billy' – a mini-boiler that heats a metal barrel into which the troops can sparingly dip a mortar case as a makeshift bucket.

Harry and his comrades savoured the moment when they could have a shower. The moment of being cool and clean was to be cherished. But it was a brief sensation. Within seconds they were enveloped in dust and dirt once more. It was the boring reality of war. But for Harry, who feared he would never see frontline service, it was thrilling.

His presence would be even more of a surprise to the Taliban – bunkered down just 500 metres, across no-man's-land, from where he patrolled. The Garmsir region is heavily infiltrated by enemy fighters, a key junction where new insurgent recruits coming over the border are 'blooded' in battle before moving north to the commercial centre of Gereshk and the Helmand capital, Lashkar Gah. Before his deployment, there had been question marks over whether the prince would ever be able to get out on patrol because of the risk that insurgents would find out he was there and step up attacks. In reality, his patrols would become part of his routine.

In a sequence of photographs taken as part of the news-blackout deal in January 2008, he was pictured patrolling Garmsir's near-deserted bazaar. There were already signs of life. On one street corner Afghan National Police were playing football with what looked like a plastic light bulb. Harry smiled and waved at them. They didn't have a clue who he was. It had to be like that. In the past members of the ANP had been suspected of tipping off the Taliban. Some had even been Taliban fighters in a previous incarnation; such is the absurdity of modern Afghanistan. 'Just walking around, some of the locals or the ANP, they haven't got a clue who I am, they wouldn't know,' Harry explained later.

As the prince patrolled outside the gates of FOB Delhi, the streets were all but deserted, with empty shops lying open, populated only by feral cats. Because they had changed hands between Taliban and Coalition control several times, evidence of destruction was everywhere. Until fierce fighting a year ago sent the civilian population fleeing, the bazaar was a bustling thoroughfare, the economic heart of southern Helmand. Already, as Harry patrolled, around 140 people had moved back into a handful of compounds at one end of the bazaar. Local Afghan police kept records of who owned which empty shop and house, ever hopeful that population would one day return.

Harry's and his comrades' foot patrols were part of a process – providing reassurance to residents. Major Mark Milford explained, 'I would love to get this place cleaned up ready to move into by the time I leave. There's still a lot of tension down here. They know that 500 metres south are the Taliban, so the Afghans are very cagey about being seen to work for the coalition.'

For someone normally recognised almost everywhere he has ever been in life, Harry clearly found the anonymity refreshing. 'It's fantastic,' he said when interviewed by John Bingham from the Press Association. 'I'm still a little bit conscious [not to] show my face too much in and around the area. Luckily, there's no civilians around here ... it's sort of a little no-man's-land.'

But the realisation that the anonymity may not last was never far away. 'I think up north, when I do go up there, if I do go on patrols in amongst the locals, I'll still be very wary about the fact that I need to keep my face slightly covered,' he said. 'Just on the off chance that I do get recognised which will put other guys in danger.'

The patrol over, the prince was back inside the base. One of the main discussions centred on how to distinguish friend from foe, civilian from Taliban gunman. It had been a major part of the prince's preparation. Among the indicators that should alert him to a possible suicide bomber were heavy sweating and an absence of body hair, as well as a refusal to respond to warning shouts. There were strict rules of engagement to obey. Warning shouts were essential. But, while nobody wanted to shoot the wrong person, equally they knew a split-second delay could cost one or one's colleague a life.

Stories of what was happening in Afghanistan had trickled back to Harry before he had been deployed. When he got there, horror stories were high on the agenda. It wasn't so much that people were being killed – he expected that – but *how* they were being killed. One incident, involving a Canadian officer, was particularly shocking. During one 'meet-and-greet' with the locals near Kandahar he took off his helmet and sat on the floor to take tea with them. He had a bodyguard with him. As they started to talk somcone came out of the group and struck an axe in his head.

Inside camp, limited water meant that, for once, the constraints of military life were cast aside and shaving was not always required. Unhampered by rules, not to mention wives and girlfriends, the men grew beards – the bushier the better. Among Muslims, they are a sign of masculinity and toughness. The camp was male-dominated. Life may be basic in the extreme, but for some it provides a rare opportunity to savour a semi-feral existence.

'Geri' Halliwell and 'Dougie' Douglass were just two of the prince's comrades-in-arms in the bloody war against the Taliban. To a man, they had nothing but praise for 'a quality bloke'. The unkempt appearance of Harry's troops may have caused surprise back home, to those used to seeing military men clean-shaven and with cropped hair. But in the gruelling Afghan desert the rules were relaxed.

Others in his battle group – Lance Corporal Frankie O'Leary, Corporal of Horse Paul Carrington, Trooper Jale 'Max' Galavakadua and Trooper Qoriniasi 'Max' Matai Loloma – were forced to endure appalling winter weather. It was hot in September when they got there, a couple of months ahead of Harry, but then the rains came and the sand turned to slush and mud, with tanks and vehicles slipping and sliding around. Then it got cold and dropped to minus 10 degrees Celsius at times, with food and water frozen.

Frankie O'Leary, a twenty-one-year-old from Lewisham in south London, praised Harry's attitude. He said, 'When a job needs doing he doesn't shout and scream at you. He just asks you to do it. It makes you want to work for the man. He's really got stuck in. He's as keen as mustard. Many times he's stood face to face with the locals, where we do hearts-and-minds stuff, giving out water rations. They didn't know who he was but Harry's one of those officers you can talk to. He's laid back and chilled out.'

The feeling was mutual. 'They were a really good bunch of guys. In the middle of the desert all you depend on is one another, to look out for each other,' he revealed later. 'You are mates, all ranks aside.' Inside FOB Delhi it was a small slice of Britain. Around it, however, lay some of the most hostile territory in Afghanistan. It was easy for the prince to imagine the once bustling bazaar that used to ring the camp.

The minaret, belonging to what once must have been a mosque, is encircled by the remains of little shop fronts. It reminded some of Harry's colleagues of the Alamo.

Work was incessant and weekends did not exist. Days and nights merged as, for men away from battle, life took on a Groundhog Day quality, monotony laced with small treats, inventive indulgences, constant jokes and banter. In their downtime, servicemen played cards, read one of the well-thumbed and out-of-date newspapers, devoured books or listened to music and the news on the radio. First-aid drills were practised and hours were spent cleaning weapons and equipment. In a world where everything else can be destroyed by sand, it's essential that rifles remain in pristine working order.

Miles to the north, at the sprawling main British base of Camp Bastion, air-conditioned tents and Internet services were provided. But in the frontline posts life was very different. Basic gyms sprang up with skipping ropes, weights made out of ammunition boxes on metal pickets and punch bags suspended from beams. In the heat of the day, some simply retired to their cot beds, encased in mosquito nets, to rest.

Sleep, Harry soon found, was the most important part of life, as the daily routine could be quite punishing, with night-time patrols and the frequent contacts at the observation posts. The daytime heat could be oppressive, so a siesta was often a wise move.

Throughout the day, there were the ubiquitous brews – tea and coffee, often of such dire quality that they were indistinguishable from each other. Sustenance came in the shape of ration-pack meals, boil-in-the-bag corned-beef hash or Lancashire hotpot, heated on open fires and laced with bottled sauces to add variety. 'It's bizarre,' Harry said. 'I'm out here now, haven't really had a shower for four days, haven't washed my clothes for a week and everything seems completely normal.' Even by military standards conditions were austere. 'I think this is about as normal as I'm ever going to get.'

With nightly temperatures plunging to minus 10 degrees Celsius, there was no heating in sleeping areas, almost no running water in camp and little shelter from the elements. At both outposts a row of angled pipes half buried in the sand outdoors, affectionately named 'desert roses', served as urinals for the men. The main toilets were the dreaded 'thunderboxes' – plywood structures with a hole cut in the centre inside flimsy wooden cubicles. At FOB Dwyer they have been aligned southward, enabling users – as the standard joke on camp goes – to 'bare your arse to the enemy'. Waste was collected in metal containers, which were then filled with kerosene and burned, offering warmth if little else for those faced with the less-than-glamorous task.

At FOB Dwyer the prospect of being paid an extra £2 per time for this task was enough to guarantee a steady stream of volunteers, while at FOB Delhi the same task was cheerfully carried out by the Gurkha troops. At FOB Dwyer a British cook worked daily wonders with ten-man ration packs producing pasta, curries and mashed potato for hungry troops in a tented cookhouse dubbed 'Hell Man's Kitchen'.

Harry had got sick of what was on offer and complained openly. He even suggested that the TV chef Jamie Oliver could be called in to do for the army in Afghanistan, by improving the 'miserable' food given to frontline troops, what he did for British schools. 'Bangers and mash with gravy in a bag would be brilliant, awesome. I don't think you can screw that up, although I'm sure someone would manage to.'

But at FOB Delhi the Gurkha fare was the envy of the Afghanistan theatre. There were regular chicken or goat curries on offer. The Gurkhas bought live chickens and roosters from the locals, slaughtering them with their distinctive machete-like *kukris* and rustling up curries on charcoal stoves in their sleeping quarters.

'What am I missing the most? Nothing really,' said Harry, sitting in his bed space. 'I honestly don't know what I miss at all: music, we've got music, we've got light, we've got food, we've got non-alcoholic drink.' Clearly conscious of his playboy image back home, he added: 'No, I don't miss booze, if that's the next question. It's nice just to be here with all the guys and just mucking in as one of the lads.'

His previous 'home', FOB Dwyer, had been a dusty and isolated outpost in the middle of the desert about 6 miles from the frontline. The soldiers there had slept in crude bunker structures built from huge 'HESCOs', blast-proof wire-mesh cages filled with rubble and topped with corrugated iron and sandbags (and named after HESCO Bastion, the British company that produces them). The only real luxury is a television screen showing British Forces Broadcasting Service (BFBS) output thanks to a satellite link.

A battery of Royal Artillery 105mm guns provided the main excitement when the order came through for a fire mission to suppress Taliban attacks on frontline British positions at FOB Delhi, further forward.

But, while conditions were basic, FOB Dwyer's remote

location meant it had been the target of attacks only a handful of times. It could not have been more different at FOB Delhi. There, troops looked out from trenches and bunkers across 500 yards of no-man's-land to the Taliban frontline.

One of the observation posts, JTAC Hill, was built on the remains of a nineteenth-century fort, used by the British during a previous involvement. Another, codenamed Balaclava, was just a few hundred yards away on the edge of Garmsir. The main regional highway stops at Balaclava; beyond that are the Taliban. 'This is the end of the road – in many ways, really,' remarked Major Milford.

Occasionally, treats from home enlivened the daily menu. The camp always came alive when the mail turned up with letters from the soldiers' loved ones, which reached FOB Delhi barely fortnightly, but each delivery was greeted with unabated delight. Then a quiet would descend over the camp while letters were eagerly read and reread and parcels opened. Sweets and treats from home were shared out and talk of home would fill the air.

The soldiers' only other contact with spouses, parents or children waiting on tenterhooks back in the UK, or at bases in Germany, was the thirty minutes they were allowed on the satellite telephone each week. Soldiers crouched in corners of the camp, seeking a better signal or a rare moment of privacy as they attempted through the crackle to reassure relatives, or simply to catch up on the everyday matters of a world that seemed light years away – birthdays that must be remembered, household bills paid, or sports results celebrated.

At night, the camp descended into darkness. The temperatures plunged. There was respite from the heat but in winter the temperatures dropped dramatically. The almost incessant thunder of artillery or mortar fire in the distance provided a backdrop.

Harry shared a room with a constantly changing contingent of Royal Artillery soldiers, alternating between stints up on JTAC Hill and the camp itself. 'This is what it's all about,' he remarked. 'What it's all about is being here with the guys rather than being in a room with a bunch of officers. I'm in here with all the guys. Most of them are artillery guys, basically doing a swap-over with the other ones on JTAC Hill, stagging on, stagging off, doing a week because it's quite a lot of graft up there.

'It's good fun to be with just a normal bunch of guys, listening to their problems, listening to what they think. And especially getting through every day, it's not painful to be here, but you are doing a job and to be with such fantastic people, the Gurkhas and the guys I'm sharing a room with, makes it all worthwhile. It's very nice to be a normal person for once. I think this is about as normal as I'm ever going to get,' he said.

In such a poignant longing to be normal, it was hard not to hear the voice of the wounded little boy who had been forced to endure both the histrionics of his troubled late mother as she coped with the torment of her life in the royal goldfish bowl, and having to deal with the shocking aftermath of her sudden death when he was just twelve years old. Normal life for both him and his older brother William was practically impossible.

To some, myself included, his words echoed those of his mother, who often complained that 'nobody understands me'. She, too, craved being 'ordinary'. It seemed an extraordinary remark. Did he really have to go halfway around the world to the most dangerous place on the planet to be himself and find normality? Was it really 'normal' to put yourself in a place where your mortality is at risk every day, where the chances of grave injury are a very real possibility?

Harry was a soldier now, and this was his new normality.

CHAPTER FOURTEEN

IN THE HEAT OF BATTLE

'The thundering line of battle stands,
And in the air death moans and sings;
But Day shall clasp him with strong hands,
And Night shall fold him in soft wings.'

FROM THE POEM 'INTO BATTLE' BY WORLD WAR I POET JULIAN GRENFELL

The Taliban firepower was deafening and relentless. Firefights had been raging all day and FOB Delhi was now under heavy attack from all sides. Observing the terrifying scenes from a nearby fortified post, Harry, JTAC Widow Six Seven, knew his pals needed close air support – and quick.

The first skirmish had happened several hours earlier, just before 10 a.m. Gurkha troops at a small British observation post in frontline Garmsir were caught up in a contact with Taliban fighters firing across no-man's-land.

The rugged British military detachment of Nepalese-born fighters took cover and then hit back decisively. They radioed for support. Royal Artillery guns answered the call, firing round after round onto pinpointed positions from over 11 kilometres away. If 'Terry Taliban', as the British forces called the religious warriors, wanted a fight, they were going to get one.

The Taliban fighters dived for cover as the terrible bombardment was unleashed. Within minutes, though, they were armed and ready again. They retaliated with RPGs and 107mm rockets showering the British encampment with lethal firepower from antiaircraft guns and AK-47s. Embedded behind 'Line Taunton', a trench system defended by a minefield, they were a determined and skilled force.

The fortification system being targeted, codenamed 'Purple', sat just 150 metres behind that Taliban frontline.

Harry had spent the previous two days monitoring Taliban movements via unmanned aerial vehicle surveillance feeds. At last, he had been cleared to call in the strikes. It was as if he were on autopilot. He patched through to Captain Ben Donberg, an American F-15E pilot cruising overhead. The pilot, from the US Air Force's 336th Fighter Squadron, based at Seymour Johnson Air Force Base, was accustomed to defending FOB Delhi, the scrappy British garrison in Helmand. As far as he was concerned, it was just another part of his Operation Enduring Freedom tours.

An adrenalin-fuelled exchange with the British officer followed. His heart pumping, Harry managed to keep his cool. It was what he had trained for and he did not want to let his men or himself down. On Harry's instruction, Ben Donberg's two-seater fighter, also carrying a weapons systems officer, Captain Ben Hopkins, streaked towards the action zone with another F-15E at its side. The soldier-prince waited for his moment.

As the firing on the ground began to subside, Harry sent the two jets off around 10 kilometres away to drown out the aircraft noise, a move that would otherwise be sure to force the Taliban to take cover. Within less than an hour, fifteen Taliban fighters had emerged and could be seen in and around the area of the bunkers. Naïvely, they thought the danger had passed.

Not taking his eyes of his computer monitor, Harry made his move. His heart still racing, he called the jets back and verified coordinates. There were to be two separate targets at opposite ends of the bunker system. Once ready, the pilots signalled 'in hot' to the prince. Decisively, he gave them the final go-ahead with the words 'cleared hot'. Grainy images from an army 'Rover' terminal screen showed what Harry saw as the pilots lined up the targets and dropped the first two 500-pound bombs.

The third strike, another 500-pound bomb, exploded moments after the first two, just as Taliban fighters emerged from cover in full view of the aircraft above. It was 30 December 2007. It would be two months before Captain Donberg and his crew realised that the voice had belonged to Prince Harry. Unbeknown to them, they had just executed the prince's first air strike.

'It was a memorable sortie, even without knowing that was Prince Harry,' Donberg said. 'No kidding. We were impressed by his proficiency level.'

Harry kept his composure despite the obvious stress in his voice, the US officer confirmed. It would be an experience Harry and Donberg, who had joined the US Air Force four years earlier, would never forget. 'I'll take this experience with me for the rest of my career, the rest of my life.'

Americans, as a general rule, love the British royals. Lady Di, as many called Harry's mother even after she married his father and became a princess, had been a US icon in life and death. Now they had another royal hero to champion, even though Harry would later try to play down his individual role on the frontline. 'Harry the hero' was a headline he wanted to avoid. 'This is a guy that didn't have to go,' said US Colonel Dan DeBree, who, at the time of Harry's tour, served as vice commander of Bagram Airfield, the nerve centre for Afghanistan air operations. 'But he was in there, in the trenches with the rank and file, doing his job.' Nobody could now deny Harry had played his part.

He had first spotted Taliban fighters moving between the bunkers two days earlier. As many as eight of the religious warriors had been seen digging trenches, identified by a lawnmower-sized Desert Hawk drone and a manned reconnaissance aircraft, which was able to watch the ground undetected by the Taliban because of its height. Harry's job of JTAC was straightforward enough on paper; but, when every decision he made could cost lives on both sides, it was nerve-racking. He was tasked with positively establishing that the figures seen moving about below were definitely enemy forces. It included carrying out a 'pattern of life' study, establishing both the movements and routines of the Taliban and being sure that there were no civilians on the ground.

On the night before his first air strike, the prince stayed at his post until well after midnight. He could not take his eyes off the screen as he surveyed movements in the area. The first pictures came from a Desert Hawk drone, which beamed back night-vision pictures dubbed 'Green Eye'. Later, two British Harrier jets flew in from the north to survey the area, picking up heat sources, including suspected Taliban and even what appeared to be a dog running around. Harry knew an enemy strike was imminent and he knew he had to be on top form for what followed.

It had become second nature. He had learned a lot in a matter of days; he had had to.

When he had first arrived his comrades had nicknamed him 'Budgie'. It was a playful dig at his age. After all, he had just replaced 'Buzzard', a veteran attack controller named after the bird of prey. Major Mark Milford of the Royal Gurkha Rifles decided a less ferocious bird name was more appropriate. The nickname stuck, but Harry soon got used to directing pilots through enemy airspace.

'When I was in the base, the major gave me the name "Budgie". I think it was his joke, stringing it in with the air thing,' Harry recalled. 'The first morning I was flapping like a budgie, so I suppose it ties in quite well. I was told to answer the phones and I had got phone calls to make as well to relevant people about organising airspace and generally finding out information,' he said.

'And they all know me as "Budgie". When this all comes out, they might think, "Ah, that's who Budgie is!" But I am literally Budgie and they can't work out what rank I am, which is quite entertaining.'

The prince would soon get used to playing down his role. The army was all about being part of a team, and he would stress time and again that he was just a cog in a wheel. Harry said in the pooled television interview: 'It's somewhat like what I can imagine World War Two to be like. It's just no-man's-land. They poke their heads up and that's it. If the guys are coming under a lot of fire, then I call the air in and as soon as the air comes up they disappear down holes or into their bunkers. My job is to get air up. They check in to me when they come into the

ROZ [restricted operation zone] and then I'm basically responsible for that aircraft, making sure it doesn't get taken out by a shell.

'Sitting in that room looking at the screen, any JTAC will tell you it's a piece of piss, really. It's when you're on the ground carrying all the kit, and, then you come under contact, you've got to type in the password. If your computer is not on already, you flip it open, get on the radio, get the jets in and you almost become like a bit of an air-traffic controller: you've got jets flying all over the place and you're trying to control them while looking at the screen, while trying to show a presence of force with your jets to get the enemy to go to cover and to keep your guys in one piece and keep safe, basically.' He made it sound simple, but it was far from simple. The pressure of working under fire should never be underestimated. What was certain is that it did not faze Second Lieutenant Wales. He was up for the fight and wanted more.

On 2 January Harry began a week at JTAC Hill. This nineteenth-century fort had been strengthened but was still pretty basic. It was known as the Taliban blooding zone, a bleak and wind-blasted place. It was the only elevated point for miles around and the Taliban had been trying to blast the British troops out of it for more than a year. A stark rule exists here: if they survive a few days trying to kill British soldiers, the warlords send them on missions further north. If they perish, they get a simple burial in the dirt of the Afghan–Pakistan border badlands. Thankfully, no British soldier in this deployment had at the time of publication been killed on JTAC Hill, despite more than a hundred assaults in the month before Harry's posting. But the almost daily defeat of the Taliban would be at no small cost: a few weeks later a Gurkha suffered serious injury after being shot in the face. There had been close calls, and Harry knew he had to be at his sharpest.

In the distance, wild dogs whined in the wind. It was the calm before the storm. Between sixteen and twenty Taliban had been spotted moving forward, preparing to attack. Harry crouched on sandbags, an open box of ammunition at the ready next to him.

Then the crack of an AK-47 rent the air. Harry gritted his teeth and prepared to open fire; he wasn't about to let them in – not on *his* watch. As a Gurkha rifleman unleashed a £65,000 Javelin missile at Taliban fighters on the edge of no-man's-land, the order went out to man the machine guns. This was Harry's chance to put his training into practice.

Wearing earplugs for protection he focused, peering through an arch of sandbags over the abandoned farmland. A shredded piece of sackcloth hanging in front of him was the only cover for his firing position. Within seconds he went into action, pumping rounds from a .50-calibre heavy machine gun from a watchtower on the top of the hill across 500 metres of cratered no-man's-land, using only distant puffs of smoke as his target.

The enemy attack was fought off within half an hour as the fighters retreated under Harry's fire. It was an exhilarating and terrifying moment at the same time. After the firefight, grinning, possibly with relief, Harry revealed, 'This is the first time I've fired a .50-cal.' It was just three weeks into his tour. Next to him a Gurkha soldier had filmed his debut on the prince's own handheld camera. Some would later dismiss the film as British propaganda.

But this was a real firefight. Just like thousands of other British soldiers in Afghanistan and Iraq, Harry could now add the clip to his private video collection filmed during his tour.

'The whole place is just deserted. There are no roofs on any of the compounds; there are craters all over the place; it looks like something out of the Battle of the Somme,' he remarked. Major Mark Milford had watched the prince in action. He had come up to the mark and the senior officer was pleased. 'This is the southern border for the coalition troops; this is about as dangerous as it can get,' he said.

His involvement in the thick of battle had left him exposed to real danger, not just for the duration of his tour of duty but for the rest of his life. In an interview, he acknowledged that his deployment to Afghanistan had increased the risk from home-grown extremists sympathetic to the Taliban. He had killed their Islamic brothers and, in their eyes, as a serving army officer he was a legitimate target. In characteristically blunt language, he said that British-born terrorists may try to 'slot' (street slang for shoot) him on his return. He shrugged off the danger, saying that, as a member of the Royal Family, he was used to threats. His remark was reminiscent of one made by his father, who famously told reporters during a trip to Spain that there's nothing you can do if your name is on the bullet. He also rejected the idea that he would have to beef up his own security on his return to Britain.

Insurgents had already gone on the record as saying the Queen, as the head of the Church of England, was the leader of a crusade against Muslims and the prince's deployment would only make matters worse. 'Once this ... comes out, every single person that supports them will be trying to slot me. Now that you come to think about it, it's quite worrying.' He laughed, albeit a little nervously. He went on, 'I think there's a lot of guys here who hopefully won't be targeted but ... now everyone will know I'm out here, no doubt I'll be a top target.'

It was about to get even more dangerous. Four days later, Harry's cover would be blown. The Australian magazine *New Idea*, a publication that had not been party to any international embargo, published an article on its website reporting that Harry had seen frontline action in Afghanistan despite opposition from the British government and members of the Royal Family. Harry was not informed of the breach. But, back at the MoD in Whitehall, it was viewed as a serious. The six SAS troopers who had acted as 'guardian angels' to the soldier-prince during his tour were alerted.

The elite soldiers flew Harry to Afghanistan in secret to help prevent news of his deployment getting out. They were not his armed guard – the prince had performed his duties like any normal officer – but the SAS unit had been on permanent 'stand-by' in case Harry needed to be extracted. Now the news was out, there were fears that the Taliban would try to locate their trophy target. A decision had to be taken at the highest level.

General Sir Richard Dannatt weighed up the situation. He knew his head would be on the block if anything were to happen to Harry, especially after the news had been made public. As a general, he was used to taking calculated risks; it went with the territory. The deal with the British media held firm. It was not reported in the mainstream newspapers. The television and broadcast media held firm too. His meetings with media executives had paid off. It was a risk, but he decided to keep Harry in theatre. (However, at this point he had not reckoned on the popularity of the US blogger Matt Drudge, who would pick up the story and run with it, as we shall see in Chapter 16.)

Three days later his Brigade commander at Camp Bastion ruled that Harry had more than passed his operational test. It was time for him to move on. His tough time in Garmsir had paid off. Now he would combine his new airstrike skills with his original role commanding tanks and going into battle. He was ordered to the war-scarred town of Musa Qala in the infamous Sangin Valley, the Taliban's deadly central heartland. The town had just been retaken from the Taliban in a massive two-week assault by US and British troops driving out 600 to 700 fighters. Harry landed at FOB Edinburgh to join a troop of Spartan reconnaissance tanks.

CHAPTER FIFTEEN

DESERT MORNING SONG

'Life's no life when honour's left;
Man's a man when honour's kept.
Nation's honour and nation's fame;
On life they have a prior claim.
When thoughts of these I do remain;
Unvexed with cares of loss or gain.
Khushal Khan Khattack, Pashto poet
and 17th Century warrior

Tears rolled down Wali Mohammed's face as much in anger as in grief. He raged that he had counted fifteen bodies of women and children on the streets of Musa Qala. They had perished as the British, American and Afghan government troops launched ferocious attacks to retake his home town. He had stayed while others fled and had watched his neighbours perish in the onslaught. Eleven-year-old Aktar Mohammed had stayed, too. Many of his family members, he claimed, had also been killed and their broken, bloody bodies lay under the dust and rubble that was all that remained of where their homes had once stood.

Taliban fighters who survived had long fled to the mountains. They would regroup and fight again. British officials insisted our troops were not responsible for the slaughter of innocent children. Two, they confirmed, had been killed – but they blamed the retreating Taliban forces for the atrocities. Jihadists warriors had forced one family at gunpoint to flee in a speeding car and race towards advancing British troops. A soldier had opened fire, thinking the vehicle was a suicide bomber. Correct procedures had been followed, the officials stressed. The truth, it seemed, was always the first casualty in war, and it was not clear who was telling it.

Most of the fighting was done in the countryside around the town, sparing Musa Qala itself. Although two soldiers were killed in the run-up to the assault, none died in the battle itself. The town, overlooked by a mountain so austere and dramatic it was known to the British soldiers as Mount Doom, had seen some of the fiercest battles involving British troops since the Korean War.

But months after the British withdrawal following the fatally flawed truce of 2006, negotiated by local Afghan authorities and the village elders, the insurgents had returned, turning the town into a symbol of their strength and a base for operations against the British across the whole of the south of the country. President Hamid Karzai could not tolerate it; nor could the Western forces there to prop up his so-called new democratic Afghanistan. So, in December 2007, the bloody battle to retake the town began. Within days, the Taliban resistance just crumbled and they headed for the hills.

Just four weeks later, Harry, strapped into a Chinook, touched down at the nearby FOB Edinburgh. All around him were biblical scenes: a herd of scrawny goats shepherded by a black-eyed boy wielding a stick; two camels, their Bedouin riders swathed in folds of white cloth, made their way across an empty plain; a chaotic weekly market held on a dry riverbed, where old men struggled to part the goats from the sheep. It had become all very familiar to the young titian-haired Second Lieutenant, now a battle-hardened officer. The fight for the town may have been over, but victory was far from certain. Hearts and minds needed to be won, and the Taliban who terrorised the surrounding villages captured or killed.

Fresh-faced soldiers, many even younger than the twenty-three-year-old soldier-prince, were given the uncomfortable task of conducting foot patrols through the narrow streets and down town alleyways. They likened the experience to 'Crossmaglen on steroids'. Locals rarely looked them in the eye. They would walk past them with their eyes firmly fixed to the ground.

It didn't exactly make the British feel welcome. Harry and his comrades had the distinct impression that the townsfolk were simply waiting to see which way the wind blew. Why shouldn't they? What was the point of committing themselves until they knew who was really in control? How could they know if the British were going to tough it out and stay or simply let the Taliban walk back in as they did before?

Harry's commanders hoped Musa Qala would become a symbol of what might be if the West could use the right mixture of force and reconstruction to help the Afghans build a better country. Initially, several hundred troops were on the streets. People who fled the town were beginning to return, but nearly all of the shops remained closed and the town showed scars from the bombardment that had driven out the Taliban. The British had offered to build a mosque, schools and a health clinic, but some locals had angrily stressed they just wanted security.

The prince's new mission was in the poppy heartland of the country's opium trade. Patrolling troops had discovered a heroin refinery in a row of derelict garages – and a stock of opium that would have produced heroin with a street value of £5 million. It was burned on a bonfire. British soldiers sheltered in the open-fronted buildings, which offered little protection against the rain, snow and intense cold – night-time temperatures often fell to minus 10 degrees Celsius.

At FOB Edinburgh, Harry was briefed fully about his new role. He was told he would be joining a troop of Spartan reconnaissance tanks and tasked with commanding a seven-strong team supporting a major US and Afghan attack to capture the remote village of Karis de Baba nearby. It was one of the places where Taliban fighters had fled, and preventing them from regrouping was seen as a priority.

Back at base, the prince enjoyed some rare downtime. Since he had arrived, he had grabbed sleep when he could. The odd hour here or there made such a difference. He had done his best to stay in touch with loved ones and family while on the frontline, but it was not always possible. Every morning he and the Toms would play touch rugby or have a kick-about using a ball made from toilet roll.

When morale was flagging, thoughts wandered to home. New technology meant communications had improved for soldiers on the frontline. But Harry had no special privileges because of his royal rank. Like everyone else, he was given a Paradigm card, which lets the soldier call home and speak for thirty minutes a week. 'It isn't great, but I think it was over the Christmas week everyone was given fifteen extra minutes, which was very nice. There was a rumour about the *Sun* giving an extra ten minutes. I refuse to accept those ten minutes,' he joked. 'I try to ring home and ring the necessary people whenever I can, once a week maybe, otherwise you just run out of minutes.'

He spoke to his family several times. For so many of the servicemen and women on the frontline, calls home boosted morale. Harry was no different. He loved being with the guys when it was flagging. He also made several emotional calls to Chelsy. Her nerves had been on edge ever since he told her he was going. Just a few days before he flew out to the conflict zone in December, the two had met in a cloak-and-dagger operation at Clarence House to say goodbye.

At the time, they were officially separated. But the enforced separation had crystallised their emotions for each other. There had been many times when the young student had sobbed down the phone. Harry would set her off because he was emotional too. By now, Harry was confident that, when he did return home after his six-month tour, they would try again to make their relationship work. Perhaps the nineteenth-century American writer Belle Boyd was right: 'A true woman always loves a real soldier.'

Chelsy was one of the privileged few who knew where Harry was. The prince had done his best to avoid letting the secret get out by telling only those who really needed to know of his whereabouts. 'No one really knows where I am, and I prefer to keep it that way for the meantime until I get back in one piece, and then I can tell them where I was. At the moment, I think they think I'm tucked away, wrapped up in cotton wool.'

His comment echoed that made by his brother William

when he was interviewed about joining the army in 2005. He had said, 'The last thing I want to be is mollycoddled or wrapped up in cotton wool. I want to go where my men go and I would want to do what they do.' For William, being the older brother, it would prove a step too far; Harry was just happy to live the dream.

When asked if William would be 'jealous' when he found out where Harry was during one of the prearranged in-theatre media interviews, the prince sidestepped the issue deftly. 'Well, he does know where I am. He's jealous anyway because I'm a JTAC and it's one of the best jobs in the army. I think there's a lot of people who disagree with that but I think there's a lot of people who would agree, mainly the JTACs. But I don't think he'll be jealous. He's a little bit upset that he can't come out here and I can, but I'm sure he'll have his time whether it's in a plane or in a helicopter ... aircraft, sorry, jet.'

Letters from home during any war have always been a lifeline. It was no different for the frontline troops almost a century after the battles of the Somme and Paschendale, when the teenage soldiers received letters from parents or sweethearts. There was always a whiff of excitement when the post arrived in Afghanistan, too. It was just that in the more remote areas it rarely came.

His lack of correspondence from back home had been a source of some irritation for the prince. At large bases, with email, Internet and land mail, there were no problems, but in distant outposts or when on reconnaissance work in the desert it was a different story. When one group of journalists arrived at a grid reference in a Chinook helicopter a week earlier, Harry's first question was, 'Have you brought any post?'

When his spirits were flagging weeks earlier, he had received a real morale boost: a letter from William. He treasured it. William wrote telling him how proud their mother Diana, Princess of Wales, would be of his serving his country. In a moment of self-doubt, it had made a huge difference. When he was handed a letter with his father's distinctive handwriting in early February, he was thrilled, too, until he realised that it was his Christmas card!

There were good reasons why post was held up at main bases. Getting it to more remote locations such as the ones Harry had served in meant that it had to be sent by helicopter. It therefore had to compete with higher priorities. Often, sacks of mail would be thrown out to be replaced by rations, ammunition and medical supplies, all listed by the officer commanding as essential on that drop.

'It's something that needs to be worked on,' Harry said critically. 'No doubt I'll be asked numerous things and it's the one thing I'll bring up – the way the guys' general morale rocks up when post comes. I've been getting post. I got a Christmas card from my dad two weeks ago and that was pretty hard to take, and I was a bit miffed.'

In truth, he did not really have time to think about his disappointment. There was always something more pressing. Similarly, although William's comments about Diana had boosted his morale, he knew he could not dwell on it. He felt she would be 'having a giggle' at his expense when things went wrong. 'Hopefully she would be proud,' he said. 'She would be looking down having a giggle about the stupid things that I've been doing, like going left when I should have gone right, finding myself in an awkward position earlier today.'

He added, 'William sent me a letter saying how proud he

reckons that she would be. You know, it's one thing that I don't necessarily think about the whole time because I've got the guys to worry about. You worry about yourself, you worry about the blokes you're looking after, you worry about the blokes that you're not even looking after. You know, at the end of the day, I'm an officer and you're supposed to be able to look after everybody and that's the way it is – you come last. So I haven't really had a chance to sit down and think about it much.'

He went on, 'I suppose it's just the way it is, there are other people out here who've lost one of their parents. I'm sure it's the same for them. If you ... think about stuff like that then you're only going to feel sorry for yourself – just get on with the job, have a laugh with the blokes; if you want to feel sorry for yourself, do it when you get back.'

He was right. There was no time to dwell on the past. He had to focus, as he would soon be engaged in a mission that would combine his new and old skills, as a JTAC and a troop commander.

Harry's job was to lie in wait outside the village and attack or capture Taliban fighters fleeing under the American onslaught. The new role meant he met lots of Afghan civilians face to face as he stopped and searched vehicles. With his light beard growth and face always slightly covered, a precaution the prince always took without thinking, he was never recognised.

In theatre, Harry explained, 'As far as I'm concerned I'm out here as a normal JTAC on the ground and not Prince Harry. When I go on patrols in amongst the locals I would still be very wary. I need to keep my face slightly covered just on the off-chance that I do get recognised, which will put other guys in danger. The great question is "Where's the Taliban?" I have asked, "Where's Bin Laden?" in the past. They just laugh. One guy said "You're too late!"'

It was here, in the remote villages outside Musa Qala on one of these patrols, that Harry had his closest shave when his convoy nearly hit a Taliban landmine. It was spotted in their path by a drone aircraft and the column was halted within a whisker of an ambush. It could so easily have been a bloodbath. The homemade mine, called an improvised explosive device or IED by the military, was constructed from an old Russian antitank shell.

Harry employed his new skills as a JTAC to save valuable hours on the operation by intercepting a helicopter carrying a Gurkha bomb-disposal team and persuading it to change its landing spot. The helicopter had been ordered to land several kilometres away to cut the risk of being mortared from the ground. But Harry managed to persuade decision makers to allow the team to land close up for the first time, promising a squadron of Spartan and Scimitar armoured vehicles as protection. 'It's rare you actually manage to change their minds,' the prince said with a smile.

The next day the situation got hotter. There was an enemy observation point the British and Americans knew about at the base of a hill. They were firing 107mm rockets continually for three or four days. The Americans had information to suggest that they were spread across through the compounds. Harry job was to clear through the compounds assisting the Americans the best he could.

'Obviously, they were a little bit more switched on than the C Squadron of the HCR [Household Cavalry Regiment] in our little mini-tanks, which they kept taking the piss out of,' he joked. They swept through and found a huge enemy OP and command centre with a 20-foot VHF antenna, both of which were used for not only long-distance communications but also to detonate IEDs by remote control from a greater distance. It was seen as a major breakthrough.

Then came the moment that would live with Harry for the rest of his life; a moment when he was exposed to the real possibility of serious injury. The Afghanistan National Army was under fire from the Taliban and taking heavy casualties. The seriously injured needed to be airlifted to Camp Bastion and Harry, as the JTAC on the ground, was tasked with calling in the Chinook for an emergency medical evacuation. Suddenly, his position came under attack from the Taliban, using 107mm Chinese-made rockets. The prince was ordered to dig in and take cover as the rockets rained down. One exploded to devastating effect a mere 50 metres from where the prince was dug in. Fortunately, he escaped without a scratch and as soon as the rocket fire ceased the prince called in the Chinook. One military source told me: 'He was lucky to have escaped without injury. It was well within shrapnel range.' The prince had remained calm under fire. He had carried out his duties precisely. But if he didn't realize before he now knew he was in a real fight. The adrenalin rush was over and he was soon back on patrol on the skirts of Musa Qala.

Harry was in his element out there. Bizarrely, he admitted later that it had been one the happiest times of his life. And sometimes, for a moment or two, he actually forgot where he was.

It was hard to imagine that he was actually in a war zone. 'It's hard to actually bring yourself back to reality and say, "No I could actually get shot at any point," just because the area itself was so nice.' The human cost of the War on Terror in Afghanistan had been terrible. But so too had destruction of the natural environment and native wildlife.

That morning Harry was astonished by what he heard when he awoke. There was not the usual sound of artillery or, worse, the eerie silence of expectation. For the first time in his tour of duty he heard the birds singing their hearts out in the middle of the desert. It was almost spiritual. Perhaps they were trying to tell him something in their morning song.

CHAPTER SIXTEEN

COMING HOME

'It's been quite difficult also having to keep quiet about the fact he was serving in that part of the world. People kept saying to me, 'You must be so frustrated about Harry not being able to serve abroad.'
PRINCE CHARLES, INTERVIEWED ON PRINCE HARRY'S HOMECOMING.

Prince Harry's heart sank when he heard the message coming over the airwaves. It may have been in code but it didn't take much for him to work that out the voices on the radio were actually talking about him. He was on 'stag duty' – monitoring the radio chatter – and within minutes his worst fears had been confirmed. He didn't know the circumstances, but it was clear his war was over.

The six SAS troopers who had acted as 'guardian angels' to the prince during his tour in Helmand had never been far away. Now they were on their way to get him out of the war zone and back home to England. There would be no time for ceremony and barely any time to say goodbye to men he had formed such a powerful bond with in just a few weeks.

Harry had known that eventually this moment would arrive. For whatever reason, his cover had been blown and now the world was beginning to find out that he was on the frontline in Afghanistan. In the careful build-up to his arrival, it had been explained over and over again that, once news of his deployment leaked, he would have to go home, not just for his sake, but also for those of the brave soldiers around him.

In his head Harry knew that this was the right way to do things and was aware of the immense and detailed planning that had gone into getting him to where he was now. But, in his secret heart of hearts, he was hoping that he could be left alone to get on with the job of soldiering. Over the previous ten weeks he had come to love this life, where he was able to put his training and discipline to the test. Here he could be a 'regular guy' and just another 'one of the lads' out doing a difficult, even dangerous, job in pretty difficult circumstances.

If he was honest, he had never known another time like it. Out there he was called 'sir' because of his army rank and because his fellow soldiers respected the job he was doing to keep them all alive. There wasn't an army of flunkies bowing and calling him 'Your Royal Highness'. In truth, he sometimes found that kind of deference cringe-making. Having men and women addressing him that way was sometimes embarrassing.

Harry wasn't boasting, but he knew he had done the job pretty damn well, so to be suddenly hauled out before the end of his official four-month tour of duty was a bitter pill for him to swallow. And it was the mark of the man he had become that he disguised the obvious hurt he was feeling and accepted that it was time for him to go.

A couple of months earlier, the elite unit of soldiers who were now pulling him out had flown Harry into the war-torn province of Helmand in secret to help prevent news of his deployment from leaking out. Harry always knew the SAS were 'on standby' but he had also been told just to get on with his job as if they were not there. If they needed to act, they would know when and how. He would just have to sit tight.

The SAS unit had never been an armed guard, shadowing the prince as he completed the tour, like the Scotland Yard personal protection officers back home. That would never have worked in a war zone, although officers from the elite unit of the Metropolitan Police had travelled to Afghanistan to assist should an emergency arise. Before his deployment, the MoD had assured Harry that he would be free to perform his duties like any other British soldier and they had been true to their word.

Chief of the Defence Staff Sir Jock Stirrup and General Sir Richard Dannatt, as head of the army, decided to pull Harry out just after midday. They felt they had no choice. They feared Harry would become a trophy target once news was out, and Taliban fighters would now be doing their utmost to find him – putting at unnecessary risk the hundreds of men around him.

The SAS unit were scrambled from their secret location in Helmand and they ran towards a waiting Chinook. The mission to extract Harry was on. Within minutes, Harry was informed officially that he was being withdrawn. He was told to get his personal belongings together, pack and be ready to leave within the hour. The young soldier had, at this stage, no idea why. He was trained to follow orders and he did so to the letter.

There were stories that his army colleagues hoisted him on their shoulders after learning he was being withdrawn. The emotional soldiers reportedly sang, 'He's ginge, he's loud, he's done us fucking proud. He's here, he's mean, his gran's the fucking Queen. Nice one, Harry.'

Harry told a different story when he was informed of the reports. 'We must have been being watched by satellite,' he said. 'No, there was nothing like that. It was literally just, no one knew about it, I just went up about an hour before I left and said, "Look, I'm off." And they all thought, "Lucky you, where are you going? Are you going back down to Garmsir?" I was like, "No, England." "Why?"

'Eventually, they clicked, but, yeah, they were upset, they were pretty depressed for me and they were just, like, "It would be nice to keep you here." But I got replaced by another JTAC, so as far as they were concerned they've got air cover. That's all they really care about, I'm sure. They're not going to miss me,' he said.

Clearly disappointed, the prince was then airlifted from the war zone. He was cheered and clapped by troopers as he departed in a bid to lift his spirits. He was then whisked by Chinook helicopter to the giant Coalition airbase on the outskirts of the city of Kandahar. If he harboured any hopes of staying and completing his tour of duty, they would soon to be dashed.

Before he boarded a flight home on board a regular RAF TriStar passenger jet, Harry spoke candidly of his regret at coming home early, and he said he would relish the chance to prove himself again in battle. 'It's something I would love to do,' he said in a pooled interview. 'I don't want to sit around Windsor, because I generally don't like England that much and it's nice to be away from all the press and the papers and the general shit that they write.'

It had all happened in what seemed like the blink of an eye. One moment the prince was planning the next attack as he hunted down the Taliban, and then he was on a flight bound for RAF Brize Norton and home. The reason was simple. While the British media – press and broadcasters alike – had adhered to the deal not to publish anything about Harry's deployment, the foreign media were a law unto themselves. What Fleet Street's editors had told General Dannatt would happen *did* happen. Everyone, including the general, had been amazed that the news had not leaked earlier.

Back in London, all hell was breaking in Fleet Street newsrooms. The influential US weblog the *Drudge Report* – whose mercurial founder Matt Drudge made his name with the 1998 scoop on Bill Clinton's relationship with the former White House intern Monica Lewinsky – blew apart the news blackout on Harry's deployment. This blog is read by millions and has credibility. General Dannatt had a problem, and so did the editors who had signed up to the deal to keep the news of Harry's deployment out of the newspapers. Matt Drudge had belatedly spotted the report in the Australian magazine *New Idea* and decided to run with the story.

It was a leak too far for the MoD, whose communications department had to field calls from journalists around the world. At the *Evening Standard*, where I was working as the royal correspondent, the editor, Veronica Wadley, decided to run with the story after getting clearance; and due to the *Standard*'s early deadlines it became the first respected newspaper to run the story, which it did under the banner headline 'Harry fights the Taliban'. In the report that I wrote with the political editor, Joe Murphy, we recorded for posterity that 'The prince is the first royal to see action for more than 25 years since

Prince Andrew flew as a Navy helicopter pilot in the Falklands conflict.' It was a historic moment.

While the mandarins at the palace and MoD breathed a sigh of relief, Harry looked the picture of despondency as he prepared to leave the war zone.

General Dannatt said he was disappointed by the foreign websites that had taken up the story but praised the 'highly responsible attitude' of the British media. Not everyone agreed, however. One respected journalist congratulated the *Drudge Report* for breaking what he called the 'British media's conspiracy of silence'.

Channel 4 News's anchor, Jon Snow, wrote on his personal website, 'I never thought I'd find myself saying thank God for Drudge.' Snow praised the *Drudge Report* for ending the 'British media's conspiracy of silence'. In his regular and popular email sent out to subscribers, Snow added, 'Editors have been sworn to secrecy over Prince Harry being sent to fight in Afghanistan & Drudge has blown their cover. One wonders whether viewers, readers and listeners will ever want to trust the media again.' Viewers were, however, angered by Snow's questioning of the media blackout, a suggestion repeated on *Channel 4 News*.

A Sue Smith, from Coventry, emailed to complain,

Tonight's show talking about a 'conspiracy of silence' and the email from Jon is so far beyond the pale I will never watch *Channel 4 News* again. By these standards you would have been notifying Hitler of all our secrets. Shameful, utterly, utterly shameful.

Another said, 'Jon Snow in one absolutely idiotic, thoughtless stupid statement has just lost *Channel 4*

News one viewer.' Other emails accused Snow of 'treason' and this outraged response in turn prompted fans of Snow to issue a flurry of emails in defence of his comments. The media row over the blackout escalated. Bethnal Green and Bow MP George Galloway was highly critical of the agreement.

'I pay for the BBC and I don't like the idea that the British media should be part of the war effort,' he said on BBC1's *Question Time*. 'Prince Harry was saying on TV that he was engaging the enemy. I don't know about you, but I have no enemies in Afghanistan and the Taliban are not the enemy for me.'

The MoD always knew there was a chance that someone in the foreign media might run the story. And on Boxing Day, eight days after Harry had been deployed CNN, the respected global TV network, telephoned James Shelley, director of news at the Ministry of Defence, to say that they knew that the prince was in Afghanistan and that they were planning to run a story on it.

If they had, it would have been a catastrophe, but Shelley, who had played a pivotal role in the news blackout, was able to broker an understanding that brought them into line with the UK media outlets. The MoD had presumed all along that people in the know would talk. They knew that soldiers might ring their families and say, 'You'll never believe who's out here.' But whom would they take it to? The MoD knew that if there was no outlet for the story, and if everyone held the line, there was a fair chance that the blackout could be maintained.

General Dannatt and Shelley thought the most challenging part of the whole arrangement would come after the story had become public. 'There were also some very surprised faces in the MoD press office, because only a few members of my team knew about the agreement before then; in fact, more members of the media knew about it than people in the MoD,' Shelley said.

'We had to ensure that everyone got what they wanted out of it, from the broadsheets to the broadcasters to the big local papers. If just one of them felt that they hadn't got enough, the whole thing would've been a failure.'

General Dannatt issued a statement in which he said,

In deciding to deploy him to Afghanistan, it was my judgement that, with an understanding with the media not to broadcast his whereabouts, the risk in doing so was manageable. Now that the story is in the public domain, the Chief of the Defence staff and I will take advice from the operational commanders about whether his deployment can continue.

But, even as the statement was being read, Harry had already been informed he was being extracted. It was not only for his safety, but the safety of the men he served alongside.

Now the news was out, everyone from his grandmother to Britain's most senior warrior praised Harry. The Queen told one pensioner when she opened a care home in Windsor that the prince had done 'a good job in a very difficult climate'. Brigadier Andrew Mackay, commander of the 7,800-strong British force in Helmand, said, 'I know from my conversations with Second Lieutenant Wales that he has flourished in this most demanding of environments, relished the opportunity to serve his regiment and his country and is deservedly immensely proud of his contribution. He shared the same risks, endured the same austerity and underwent the same fears and euphoria that are part of conducting operations in this environment.

'Like every other returning soldier who has undergone or experienced intense operations, Harry will now need some time to reflect on his experience, remain close to his regiment, spend time with his family and friends and enjoy some well-earned leave. We wish him well.'

Perhaps Harry would have been most cheered by the plaudits he won from his own frontline comrades. 'Damn right, respect to the bloke for getting on the ground,' one wrote on a forces website. 'Well done Ginge!' another wrote.

One soldier confirmed that Prince Harry had been on active service throughout his ten weeks in southern Afghanistan and had not been kept away from the Taliban. 'Well done, and all I'll say is he hasn't sat in Bastion [Camp Bastion, the British main base in central Helmand Province] for three months,' he wrote.

'No argument from me,' another soldier wrote. 'I consider it a shame that this got reported, it will make him a more valuable target for mad fools. OTOH [on the other hand], it does show that the Royal Family is more in touch with the reality facing British people than anyone in government.'

One soldier said that it was a 'smack in the face' for the Taliban. Another comment seemed to sum up the view of the majority about the way that the story was leaked, first by the Australian magazine: 'It had to be a frigging convict that broke the story, nice one wankers.'

Within minutes of the news breaking the MoD's top

commanders were left in no doubt that they had made the right decision to bring Harry home. In a chilling message to Britain's soldiers, the fanatics' chief spokesman Qari Yousef Ahmadi said, 'We are trying to find him. Prince or no prince, we will keep looking for him and we will increase our attacks on all the soldiers.'

Messages were posted on a password-protected al-Qaeda forum, al-Ekhlaas, calling for Prince Harry to be beheaded and a video of his murder to be sent to the Queen. Arabic news items and photographs of the prince on duty in Helmand were added to the jihadi sites. One posting said, 'Nothing will break the heart of his grandmother but only if she loses him. My dear brothers in Allah, carry on provoking to kidnap this precious infidel.'

The Taliban also vowed to step up attacks on British forces because of the prince's deployment. 'Prince Harry's presence in Afghanistan encourages our fighters to launch more attacks on British Forces,' Zabihullah Mujahid, a spokesman for the Taliban told *The Times* in London by telephone from an undisclosed location. 'The Royal Family is now directly participating in the aggression against Muslims.'

Prince Harry acknowledged that on his return to Britain he could be a 'top target' for home-grown jihadists who were sympathetic to the Taliban. He vented his frustration at being forced home by telling another soldier, 'I'm fucking pissed off.' But his disappointment was short-lived. As he boarded the TriStar to take him home he had a rude awakening. On board, returning from the war zone, were two seriously injured soldiers. One had lost two limbs – left arm and right leg – and another had been saved by his friend's body, which was in the way, but took shrapnel to the neck. Both were out cold throughout the whole of the flight.

'Those are the heroes,' Harry said. 'Those were guys who had been blown up by a mine that they had no idea about, serving their country, doing a normal patrol. The bravery of the guys out there was humbling. I wouldn't say I'm a hero. I'm no more a hero than anyone else. If you think about it there are thousands and thousands of troops out there.'

The injuries to Marine Ben McBean, one of the injured servicemen, left a deep impression on the prince. 'They were essentially comatose throughout the whole way,' he said.

'But thanks to the skills and drills and professionalism of the ... team and all the medics, going from Stage One all the way back to the medics that check them out at Birmingham [Selly Oak Hospital, where British military casualties are treated] and hand them over, and hand them over, and hand them over – everyone on that whole stream – I would say they were heroes, they're keeping people in one piece and essentially saving lives.

'I was a bit shocked because ... it is a bit of a choke in your throat because you know that it's happening. There's a lot of time when you are actually in theatre that it's not really mentioned that much and you just hear about it when there's an op minimise [which effectively means that someone has died and that all communication, phone and e-mail with family at home is cut] or something like that, you know that something has happened somewhere.

'To actually be on a plane and sort of wait for whatever it was, an hour and a half, two hours at Kaf [Kandahar] for them to be loaded on – it wasn't as though everyone was like, "Uh, you know. I really want to get home." It's completely understandable that we had casualties to put on there. And I'm not entirely sure how many there were but there were two guys who were essentially critical.

'And it was, you know, it was hard because it was a time when you wanted to talk to them and just find out how they were. Because a typical English, or British, soldier would just turn round and go, "Oh, I'm fine, I'm fine, I've lost my arm; I didn't like that arm, anyway" – or something like that.

'And the guy who took the shrapnel in the neck, when he was choking with blood, just grabbed the piece of shrapnel and said, "Put that in a pot, I want it as a souvenir." That's just the way it is and the bravery of the guys out there is just humbling, it's amazing. There were a lot people in a worse situation than me, that's for sure. And all the infantry out there are the guys who need recognition.'

At 11.29 a.m., the RAF TriStar jet bringing home around 170 men, including the prince, touched down at RAF Brize Norton, Oxfordshire. The soldier-prince was home and, no matter how hard he tried to avoid it and rightly point out that it was others and not he who deserved praise, the phrase 'Harry the hero' was one that would stick. Even if he did not want the celebrity, the MoD and the palace would be happy to lap it up.

CHAPTER SEVENTEEN

WAR IS OVER

'When the days of rejoicing are over,
When the flags are stowed safely away,
They will dream of another wild 'War to End Wars'
And another wild Armistice day.'
FROM THE POEM 'ARMISTICE DAY, 1918' BY RUPERT GRAVES

Clutching his desert helmet, his rucksack tossed over his right arm, Harry cut a forlorn figure. His head bowed, not once did he break into a smile as he descended the steps of the aircraft at RAF Brize Norton. While most of the other 170 servicemen and women might have cheered as the RAF TriStar touched down on the airstrip on 1 March, Harry – dressed in desert combats and still craving the anonymity that came with serving in Afghanistan – was left to ponder what might have been.

There was no time for self-pity. He and the other servicemen were left in no doubt how lucky they had been to get home in one piece. The flight had earlier landed in Birmingham so that the two seriously injured soldiers could be taken to Selly Oak Hospital. The Musa Qala desert dust may have still been in his boots, but already the memory of his experiences had begun to fade.

His father and brother had been waiting patiently at the

base. The world's media were there, too, anxious to film their new royal hero. Both Charles and William were delighted to see him back safe, but also shared his disappointment at his having been withdrawn early. 'The conversation was "Hello, how are you? There's food." "Thank you very much." Wham, straight into it. And I sat down in a chair,' Harry said. 'It was just very nice to see them, just a shame that it wasn't in the circumstances I would want it to be in; but you can't be upset about being home, even if it is winter or England. It was just your normal parent-to-son or brother-to-brother conversation: "Welcome back; how was it?"' he added.

Charles also agreed to speak to the waiting media. It is not something the prince relishes – perhaps because it is more in keeping with the duties of a politician and not a future king – but it was part of the media deal his advisers had signed up to. The prince said he was 'enormously proud' of his son and said he now understood what families and loved ones endured when soldiers were serving abroad. 'As you can imagine, it's obviously a great relief to see him home in one piece,' he added. But at least now that the secret was out he did not have to keep quiet about it to his own friends.

Charles described the homecoming as an 'immense blessing' but said he was 'frustrated' that Harry had been forced to return home before his fourteen-week tour was complete, adding, 'I feel particular frustration that he was removed unexpectedly early. He had been looking forward to coming back with the rest of his regiment.'

His thoughts again turned to the soldiers serving in 'impossible conditions'. 'We don't often appreciate what the people in the armed forces are doing putting up with impossible conditions, being shot at or rocketed at and goodness knows what. The fact they do this with incredible humour and dedication is extraordinary. With Harry's own plane coming back just now, they had to stop and drop off two badly wounded people who had been blown up by mines. It brings home just how hazardous it is – and also people who are being wounded and injured all the time that we don't hear about.'

Harry was still in a sombre mood when he gave his final interview. On fighting the Taliban, he said, 'You do what you have to do – what's necessary to save your own guys. If you need to drop a bomb, worst-case scenario, then you will, but that's just the way it is. It's not nice to drop bombs. But, to save lives, that's what happens.' Harry said he had achieved what he set out to do, and that was to lead men in battle. 'As far as I'm concerned, it was mission successful, because the main crux of it was to lead a troop,' he said.

When asked whether it was one of the happiest times of his life, he replied, 'Yes, probably. It was fantastic. It was an opportunity that I was wanting to do the whole time, and to be able to do it – I was hugely grateful for having the opportunity. I did enjoy it a little bit more than I suppose I should. Not in a sick way but, no, I enjoyed being out there, I suppose. Every element had something different about it. But actually being out in the middle of nowhere, with the stars out ... it was just a fantastic place to be.'

Describing his feelings at seeing his tour cut short because of unexpected publicity, he said, 'I didn't see it coming. It's a shame. *Angry* would be the wrong word to use, but I am slightly disappointed. I thought I could see it through to the end and come back with our guys and the colonel himself. But I'm back here now and I suppose, deep down inside, it's quite nice. I'm looking forward to having a bath. But I would like to have stayed back with the guys.'

Through gritted teeth, as if under orders, Harry thanked the British press. 'I was surprised by the way the British media kept to their side of the bargain. I hate to say it but, no, I'm very grateful for that and thank you to all the British media for keeping their mouths shut. And I know for a fact that there was stuff they did behind the scenes to stop stuff coming out, which was massively kind of them. But at the same time it doesn't surprise me that once again it comes to the media, foreign media, that has once again spilled the beans, so yes it's a shame, but to be expected, I guess.'

He did not want to go into the details about the *Drudge Report*, but his disappointment was obvious. 'I don't know much about it and I don't really want to know much about it. But whatever has happened has happened and, as I said, it doesn't surprise me. There's always someone out there who is willing to ruin the party but, well, job's done.'

Harry recalled his final farewell to his men. 'Yeah, no, that wasn't great, as any person [knows] who gets pulled early for whatever reason – whether it's a compassionate case ... there's a lot of guys who get pulled for compassionate and they want to go back home and make sure everything is all right; but, at the same time, once you sort of leave the zone then you're going to miss all the guys. You find yourself mucking in and being great mates with the most bizarre people.'

But it was not all PR puff. Harry could not sidestep the big issue that a member of the Royal Family had been

actively engaged in killing. He had been filmed firing a
weapon and dropping bombs. What goes through your
mind when you have to do something like that? Harry
paused for a second to collect his thoughts. 'It's war, it's
hell, but, no, I don't know, you do what you have to do,
what's necessary to save your own guys.'

Then, for Harry at least, came the killer question. Was
he concerned that his fighting days may now be over? It
was something he had been mulling over from the moment
he left Kandahar. 'I hope not. I hope that this has now been
proven that the system can work and the British press go
along with the deal. Everything in place has proved that it
can actually work. So I don't see why it can't work again.
I know there's a lot of people thinking, "Well, you've done
it once, now you've got the medal; why would you ever
want to go back again?"

'I think at the moment, as far as I see it, I'm going to wait
for the colonel to get back and sit down and talk to him
and find out what the options are, what he's offering me as
a troop leader, as an FAC [forward air controller], and to
see how things go between now and whenever D Squadron
get back with 16 Brigade [the end of the next six-month
troop rotation]. But, as far as I see it, yeah I would love to
go back out and I've already mentioned it to him that I
want to go out very, very soon, just because, as I said in an
interview ages ago, being an FAC you are an asset, but
there's all sorts of possibilities that will arise, but I don't
intend on leaving the army.

'But ... as everyone will say to you if you ask them, once
you're back from operations everything is a bit of an
anticlimax. You go back to your unit and there you are,
day in, day out, the same routine, nothing changes, and

that's the way it is, nothing changes, at least in operations – then you are kept on your toes the whole time; that's what guys join up for I guess, that adrenalin.'

It hadn't been his most inspired interview. Indeed, it was in stark contrast to the enthusiasm he had shown when speaking to the media sent to cover the pooled reports in theatre. But, once it was over, so too were his commitments with the MoD as far as the media were concerned, and he looked relieved. Harry then led out his father and casually dressed brother to the waiting Audi estate. William and Harry loaded all the kit into the back before being driven away to nearby Highgrove.

Harry's immediate future in the army was still unclear. Although he had stressed his desire to serve again, that was out of his hands. He was allowed to go on leave for about three weeks before returning to his unit to continue his regimental duties. General Sir Richard Dannatt went on record to say Harry would not be expected to return to a war zone for another twelve to eighteen months. He went on to praise the prince as a 'red-blooded young man' and an 'enthusiastic' officer. And, while he accepted that he would be disappointed at having to return to the UK, the general added that, after his leave, Harry would return to his unit, the Blues and Royals, and continue developing his career as a young officer. Harry had already requested a return to Helmand with his regiment later in the year, but that had been turned down.

However, there was some good news for the prince. The general added that Harry would be promoted from cornet, or second lieutenant, to lieutenant on 1 April 2008. It has emerged that he came third out of a class of eighteen students when he was training to become a forward air controller.

The Prime Minister, Gordon Brown, hailed Harry too. 'I think the whole country is going to be delighted that Prince Harry has come back safely, that his security has been protected. We are very grateful to him for all the work he has done in Afghanistan – very grateful to all the soldiers in Afghanistan.'

No sooner had the royal car pulled away from the RAF base on Harry's return from Afghanistan than the backlash had begun. Initially, the press couldn't get enough of 'Harry the hero'. 'One of our boys,' proclaimed a *Sun* front page. 'Our army of readers salutes you, Harry,' added a souvenir poster across the centre spread. He had 'killed up to 30 of the enemy' and had shown 'enormous courage. He came under enemy rocket, mortar and machine-gun fire almost every day.'

'Harry and the Gurkhas give the Taliban a pasting', announced the *Express*. He was 'fighting the fanatics', advised the *Mail*. Harry was quoted as explaining that 'you are doing a job and it is all worthwhile.' Some papers gave the story a dozen pages. Some respected figures dismissed Harry's war as a 'blatant PR stunt'. The former editor of the *News Statesman* and *Independent on Sunday*, Peter Wilby, said he believed the British media had been 'suckered' into the news blackout deal and the subsequent gushing praise that was heaped on the prince on his return once he was safely back home.

Writing in the *Guardian*, Wilby pulled no punches. He wrote,

Kings and princes used to go into battle at the head of their soldiers, standards flying. Nobody thought it right to hide Henry V or Richard III while they were doing battle with the enemy. But the modern military wants the symbolic benefits of royal leadership without undue risk to the royal personage. In the case of Prince Harry, the Ministry of Defence had its cake and was allowed by the media to eat it as well. To my mind, this was propaganda for a war of dubious legitimacy and declining public popularity. The positive publicity for the Afghan war and the Royal Family – both of which are opposed by a significant proportion of the country – was priceless. The access to Prince Harry was inevitably controlled and material pooled so that all outlets had roughly the same story. It is an example of what Nick Davies, in his new book *Flat Earth News*, calls 'churnalism', whereby journalists faithfully reproduce a version of reality that has been pre-packaged by public relations. Were we going to hear anything from Harry about shortages of equipment, the justice of the war, or the likelihood that it will never be won? Of course not.

Fleet Street editors and broadcasters were accused of dealing another blow to genuinely independent journalism and to the long-term credibility of the media. How could Harry really be an ordinary soldier? The idea, commentators argued, was preposterous. He was simply a pawn in a PR game. It is true that Harry's frontline service had given the army the glamour it might otherwise lack. There had also been the added benefit that his presence and commitment had boosted morale of the serving soldiers.

The controversial former Labour MP George Galloway, who now represented his Respect Party in East London, was firmer, accusing the press of a collusion that embeds journalism in the sewer of state spin. He wrote on his internet blog,

So the greatest collusion of all by the media is in perpetuating the myths of this war and in helping to craft the perfect recruitment poster. It is better than Kitchener's 'Your country needs you'. Skilfully and chillingly, it speaks to this century and through the most modern media. It is going to play an enduring role in prolonging this futile adventure, and perhaps starting others, in a country which British armies have three times before staggered out of in defeat, leaving so many of their number behind. No one, not even Alexander the Great, has successfully occupied Afghanistan; and Harry, whatever you think about him, is certainly no Alexander the Great.

Back at Highgrove, his father's country home, Harry sank into a deep, hot bath. He was a prince again with the privileges of his royal rank. Everything was in its place, organised to perfection by dedicated royal servants. He could have forgiven himself a smile as he sank down deeper in the bath. He was filthy, by his own admission, and, despite his disappointment at his early homecoming, a long soak was some compensation. Soon, he would be reunited with Chelsy. His absence really had made both their hearts grow fonder. He couldn't wait to see her.

Outside in the lush Gloucestershire countryside he could hear the birds singing again, just as they had in the Afghan desert. The sound of artillery fire and the frontline banter of his comrades now seemed a distant memory.

CHAPTER EIGHTEEN

REAL HEROES

'The real heroes of this war are the great, brave, patient, nameless people.'
WHITEHALL REID, AMERICAN POLITICIAN
AND EDITOR (1837–1912)

Harry might have been expected to put his feet up and relax after ten weeks on the frontline in Afghanistan. But, by his own admission, home is not always his favourite place, even though he is an English prince by birth. 'I generally don't like England that much and, you know, it's nice to be away from all the press and the papers,' he admitted when interviewed.

Perhaps it was a little unwise, particularly as his family's privileged existence depended entirely on the goodwill of the people whose country he professed not to like. One cannot imagine the Queen or Prince Charles ever saying they did not like the country they have declared it is their life's duty to serve.

But who could really blame him? Since he was born, Harry has been centre stage, his life played out in public, his every move scrutinised, debated and often criticised, at times unfairly. Such is the poor publicity he generated that, before he bravely served his country as a frontline soldier, many had exhausted their patience with him and his party antics. They had dismissed him as yet another playboy prince with little or no substance.

Perhaps Harry had simply failed to articulate his feelings about his country. Or maybe it was just a slip of the tongue by a disgruntled young man who had been forced to return home by a media leak and forced to abandon his dream – maybe forever? Whatever the reason behind his ill-judged remarks, within days of his return Harry was jetting off again. He was pictured in the newspapers in the heart of Africa, showing the world where he preferred to be. He and Chelsy, their romance back on, escaped aboard a rickety houseboat along the Okavango Delta, one of Africa's last wild places. Every year, summer rains falling 1,000 miles away on the Angolan highlands surge down the Okavango River to create a miraculous oasis in the northern Kalahari. These seasonal floods arrive in the middle of Botswana's dry season, in the African winter months of July and August.

Entering the delta on the north-western side in an area known as The Panhandle, the flood waters fan out through the dense papyrus beds, creating a hippo heaven of languid lagoons and crystal channels. The huge area spans more than 10,000 square miles of forests and floodplains strewn with islands in numbers beyond counting.

Some of the islands are little more than old termite mounds, shaded by a single palm tree. Others are bigger than Greater London. To the north lies the Moremi Game Reserve, home to huge herds of elephant and buffalo and a refuge for all kinds of predators from lion and leopard to the highly endangered African wild dog. Maun, a dusty little town on the edge of the delta, is where all Okavango safaris begin.

Once again, Harry was sleeping under the stars, as he had done in the Afghan desert, but this time his life was not in danger and he had the woman he loved at his side. He was not concerned with sniper fire or antipersonnel mines hidden beneath the desert sand, just the long lenses of the paparazzi. For an idyllic month the couple escaped to Botswana, in a tent for two perched on the roof of their cruiser, a love boat called the *Kubu Queen*. It was very basic and looked as if it might sink at any moment. It was perfect place for the young couple to spend uninterrupted quality time together.

Both would have preferred to be totally alone; but, for now, he was a royal again, not an officer protected by his brothers-in-arms, and the inevitable Scotland Yard bodyguard had to accompany him as well as the captain of the vessel who would guide them. They were discreet but it was a reminder to Harry that, no matter how much he craved anonymity, he would, like his mother, always be a member of the royal family. It was as if the couple were recreating the roles played by Humphrey Bogart and Katharine Hepburn in the classic 1951 movie *The African Queen*. The message they were sending was clear: the romance was back on track and the hero's African heiress was, as far as he was concerned, his queen.

They enjoyed speedboat jaunts in one of two craft towed behind the *Kubu Queen*. In between their adventures, they cooked their meals over an open fire on deck. At night they climbed a tin ladder to the houseboat's roof – and their flimsy love nest.

Each morning Harry and Chelsy rose late and climbed

down an aluminium ladder to the main deck, where they cooked their own breakfast on a small gas cooker. Harry's customary breakfast of mashed biscuits, jam and margarine in Helmand seemed a lifetime ago. The rest of their day was spent lazily cruising up and down the waterways, normally with a can of beer and a cigarette in hand. The area was teeming with crocodiles, some up to 18 foot long, which frequently come onto land to take cattle that stray too close to the water's edge. Both knew they were experiencing something really special. It was, they knew, one of the most beautiful places on Earth, unspoiled and seen only by the most intrepid travellers.

Wearing a revealing black Billabong bikini, Chelsy dragged heavily on a cigarette as she soaked up the sun. She had grown up in Africa and appeared to take little interest in the wildlife of otters and fish eagles around them. On another day they took a small speedboat to visit a watering hole used by hippos. On the way back, Harry took over the steering wheel, laughing and joking with his Scotland Yard Protection Officer as he guided the craft confidently with one hand.

The inevitable warning letter from royal solicitors Harbottle & Lewis followed, complaining about the photographs taken with long-distance lenses. The pictures were of a private holiday and should not have been published, they said. But they were clearly important images, the first of the third in line to the throne together with his girlfriend since they split. The newspapers felt it was worth the risk.

Harry and Chelsy knew their holiday was newsworthy but were happy to take the risk of being detected, determined to rekindle their romance after a painful ten weeks apart. Clearly, as a couple they had a lot to talk about, which was why Chelsy agreed to go. After a romantic month together they knew they were right for each other and, despite their comparative youth, many inside Clarence House and Buckingham Palace would not bet against a possible future engagement.

One senior member of the Royal Household and a long-serving courtier admitted that the Prince of Wales believed Chelsy was 'terrific'. While he acknowledged that Harry was still relatively young to be thinking of marriage, he reported a significant shift in the attitude of palace courtiers towards the African heiress. 'For a long time people did not take the romance that seriously. They regarded it as a youthful relationship that would pass. But clearly, despite their being quite young, they are in love and depend upon each other.' What about a future marriage? 'I think it's a little early for that, but only a fool would rule it out. The Prince [of Wales] thinks she is terrific.'

Comparisons with William and Kate Middleton's relationship are inevitable. But, clearly, the palace mandarins are beginning to take Chelsy more seriously. In the past at royal events, including family marriages and holidays, Kate was expected to be on the guest list, but Chelsy was not. Friends said that, although there are no immediate marriage plans, Harry has been calling her 'wifey' and had talked openly about wanting six children. She apparently played along with it by dubbing him 'hubby', 'They think it's hilarious and have been falling about laughing about it,' one of their circle said. 'But it really isn't serious. They both think they're a bit young for marriage and all that it entails.'

While the couple unwound in the African sunshine, back home the backlash against Harry's war was still raging. After the initial jingoistic euphoria that accompanied the prince's return, after a period of reflection cooler heads began to prevail. And it was not just the usual left-wing politicians and antiwar campaigners who spoke out. Former soldiers such as Afghanistan veteran Leo Docherty criticised the British military campaign in Helmand.

Writing in the *Independent* newspaper, he said,

Rather than highlighting the appalling truths about the war in Helmand, the media, dazzled by the heroic ideal that Prince Harry so perfectly embodies, perpetuate the myth that this is a just war fit for heroes. The frenzy of coverage in the papers was facile: 'Watch Prince Harry fighting in Helmand,' proffered one broadsheet website. This is war reduced to entertainment, willingly ignorant of the truth that young men like Harry, both British and Afghan, are dying violent pointless deaths in Helmand Province. Outrage is the only response to this, not entertainment. Prince Harry won't have the opportunity to make a proper judgement about the war in Helmand.

After 10 weeks, six short of his planned stay, he's returning home, a pin-up hero yet an exploited victim of the media circus that drove him to seek 'normality' in Helmand in the first place. The media he blames for hounding his mother to her death have stripped him of his professional *raison d'être*. Coming home will be a blow. But this is war, not therapy. It's a war worth fighting, but it's a war worth getting right, which we're not doing at the moment. Let's hope those troops who have served alongside Harry and have months still to go get the chance, like our young Prince, to come home soon.

The brilliant war correspondent and former newspaper editor Max Hastings echoed the sentiment in the *Daily Mail*: 'The cost of acknowledging defeat by the Taliban is too high for the Western Alliance to contemplate. But officers on the ground recognise that present policies are getting nowhere and unlikely to do so.'

Was Harry used as a PR missile to bolster flagging public support for a war that some believed it is impossible to win? While nobody was advocating a full-scale withdrawal on the Soviet scale, others questioned the commitment to a conflict so far away, and one that conservatively could take a quarter of a century to resolve.

But these were issues for people far higher up the food chain than Harry. He was a soldier who just wanted to serve. He had already had a request to go on tour again and been turned down. Realistically, he could not expect another tour of duty for at least a year maybe eighteen months. In reality, he knew the chance might never come again. He was not somebody who would sit around and mope. If his experience on the frontline had taught him anything it was to realise he was only a small part of a much bigger picture. The powers that be knew he wanted to serve again; now, the ball was in their court.

What concerned him was the welfare of the men and women he had served with, shoulder to shoulder, in Afghanistan. On his return, he and William spent hours discussing his experiences. William was eager to hear everything. While the brothers laughed about Harry's new hero status, what emerged was a determination to help the real heroes, the ordinary men and women permanently injured serving their country on active duty. Both brothers agreed to do something positive for their comrades. They could stay out of politics but still make a significant difference. Their mother, one of the greatest humanitarians of the twentieth century, had shown them that.

She had always taught them that anything was possible; now it was their chance to step up to the table and prove their worth.

The media just seemed happy to have their playboy prince back. A night out at one of his old haunts, the Mahiki in the West End, inspired headlines such as 'The prince of Clubs is back'. Accompanied by his cousins, Princesses Beatrice and Eugenie, Harry enjoyed his first big night out on the town since his return from the frontline. They were joined by Holly Branson, daughter of Virgin tycoon Sir Richard, wearing a shimmering purple maxi dress.

Before arriving at the Mahiki, the royal group had been in east London for a fundraising night in memory of the princes' friend Henry van Straubenzee, who was killed in a car crash in December 2002. William and Kate had enjoyed a meal with them, watched a burlesque show and kissed on the dance floor at the fundraiser. When they arrived outside the Mahiki, however, unlike Harry and the rest, they decided to call it a night and ordered their car to drive on home.

If the waiting paparazzi were expecting to snap the old Harry, furious at their presence, they were wrong. His holiday and his wartime experience had mellowed him, maybe forever. When you've faced the Taliban, perhaps the night owls who take pictures for a living from London's pavements no longer have the same impact. Whatever the reason, Harry just walked calmly past them, barely acknowledging their existence, and into the waiting car.

He had other things on his mind. He and William were busy working on a new initiative that they hoped would make a real difference to the lives of our wounded servicemen and woman. Quietly, behind the scenes, they had agreed to back a major event in the City to support Britain's war heroes, becoming joint patrons of the City Salute, a sunset pageant on 7 May in front of St Paul's Cathedral to help raise money for injured servicemen and women and their families. The aim was to raise money for vital rehabilitation facilities. The event would include the band of the Royal Marines marching through Temple Bar, ceremonial troops and armoured vehicles of the Household Cavalry, an RAF fly-past and a *son et lumière* at St Paul's Cathedral.

Some of the money raised would go to Help for Heroes – the charity set up by former soldier and cartoonist Bryn Parry to support wounded forces personnel. Cash would also go to the Soldiers, Sailors, Airmen and Families Association and to Headley Court, the Defence Medical Rehabilitation Centre in Surrey. It was to be the brothers' first joint patronage as well as their first official joint engagement, and it would prove to be one that would stir the emotions of them both.

In smart suits and sporting their Guards Regimental ties, Harry and William arrived at Headley Court on 21 April. Inside, Harry went straight to one wounded soldier, one of the men he had called a real hero. His words were simple, upbeat even. 'Hi, I'm the guy who was on the plane with you. I was staring at you for half an hour. I'm Harry. A real honour to finally meet you properly,' he said. 'I can't believe you're standing up, it's fantastic.' Royal Marine Ben McBean had made an incredible recovery after losing his left arm and right leg in Afghanistan. The twenty-one-year-year old was moments from death when he returned home on the same flight as Harry seven weeks before.

'Harry came rushing up to me as soon as I walked in,' McBean recalled. 'It's fantastic. We had a good laugh together, and William was really nice, too. They're both very easy to talk to, just regular guys, really, because they're also servicemen like us. It's obvious they really care about the wounded and what happens to them, and that's good to know.'

McBean – who wore a Help for Heroes wristband for the meeting – told of his delight at mastering his artificial leg. He said, 'I'm over the moon, because I'm free again. I've always been a really active person, so being mobile again means so much to me. My next target is to get my new arm and learn how to use that, too. Then, next year, I'm going to run the London Marathon to raise money for Help for Heroes, for all the blokes who are still in a bad way, including guys I was in hospital with and who are sadly still there.'

Ben, part of 40 Commando based in Taunton, Somerset, even had to fight off the superbug MRSA. 'There's always someone worse off than you – that's what you have to remember. Headley Court is a brilliant place because it makes you realise that, if they can do it, you can do it. So you just crack on.'

The brothers spent two hours chatting with servicemen. They included Lance Bombardier Ben Parkinson, the most badly wounded British soldier ever to survive, after an Afghan landmine tore off both his legs and left him with thirty-seven other wounds. Also there was twenty-four-year-old Marine Mark Ormrod, who trained with Harry before going to Afghanistan. Mark lost his right arm and both his legs in a landmine blast during a routine patrol on Christmas Eve. And he said the royal visit meant so much to the patients because Harry himself had 'been there, seen and done it'.

Harry had told his commanding officers that he had to go to Afghanistan so that he could look his brother soldiers in the eye. He needed their respect if he was to continue in the chosen career he loved. At Headley Court he had achieved just that. It takes a soldier to know the fear every frontline fighter faces – and the courage it takes to overcome it. Harry showed real warmth as he greeted Ben McBean, as he took his first steps since stepping on a landmine in Afghanistan. Harry was as stunned as the medics by the determination of the man he had called a 'real hero.'

Ben's story was truly heroic – but not unique. Scores of British servicemen had returned to Britain after being terribly wounded fighting for their country. Others had not been so lucky. Harry knew his frontline experience could boost the morale of the injured and the families who had lost loved ones. But he also knew he could help provide his wounded comrades with the support and nurturing they deserved to rebuild their lives, shattered by horrific injury. He could make a difference at home, as well as on the frontline.

Lance Sergeant Adam Ball, aged twenty-three, who also lost a leg in Afghanistan, was impressed by William and

Harry. He believed that, even though it was only a two-hour visit, it had boosted the morale of the men. He said, 'I'm happy the princes have come today. It's good that they come and show an interest in what we're doing and see how we're getting on. Harry knows the ins and outs. It's more like talking to an officer than talking to a royal.'

Whether he liked it or not, Harry was now both prince and officer, and he would have to learn to combine both roles from now on.

POSTSCRIPT

The legacy of heroes is the memory of a great name and the inheritance of a great example.

BENJAMIN DISRAELI (1804–1881)
BRITISH STATESMAN AND AUTHOR

His smile said it all. As the Princess Royal, colonel of his regiment the Blues and Royals, moved along the line, newly promoted Lieutenant Harry Wales tried his best to hold a serious expression. She stopped briefly to talk to senior officers before reaching her nephew who saluted her. Then the princess, wearing gloves, pinned a campaign medal to Harry's chest. The prince could not resist breaking into a grin. The two shared a private joke and his face flushed a little red. Although most on parade had completed the four month tour, Harry had qualified for the decoration as he served more than the minimum four week period required. At that moment Harry knew he had achieved something nobody had really thought possible and now he had the medal – the Operational Service Medal for Afghanistan – to prove it.

Moments earlier, as the parade arrived, led by the band of the Blues and Royals, spontaneous applause and cheers rang out from around 600 family and friends who had gathered inside a hangar at Combermere Barracks in Windsor to watch the ceremony where 170 members of the Cavalry regiment were being decorated. Dressed in his desert fatigues, topped off by his dark blue beret, Harry stood to attention in the front row as the official royal party – including his father and brother – arrived. It was an historic moment. Not since his uncle Prince Andrew had received the South Atlantic Medal with the rosette in 1982 for his role in the Falklands war, had a British royal prince been decorated for active service.

There was another first that day; and one that could ultimately be of huge significance to the young officer's future. Sitting alongside Prince William and Prince Charles was Harry's girlfriend Chelsy Davy. In a fitted cream jacket and brown moleskin skirt, she confidently took her place in the royal ranks – the first time she had joined the family in such a public way. Her appearance made many commentators sit up and take notice. They now believed a future wedding was a serious possibility despite the couple's relative youth. The next day the *Daily Mail* newspaper could not resist making Chelsy the focus of the story, publishing a photograph of her on the front page under the headline 'Chelsy's royal engagement (not that sort!)'

After the brief ceremony Harry marched with his comrades through the Windsor streets in the shadow of the castle that is his grandmother's favoured royal residence. They headed to the garrison church, Holy Trinity, for a service of thanksgiving. As prayers were said, undoubtedly some of those present spared a thought for Trooper Ratu Babakobau, a 29-year-old Fijian who had been serving in

Helmand with the Household Cavalry. His death took the number of British military fatalities in Afghanistan since the start of operations in November 2001 to 95 souls. The Reverend Duncan MacPherson, the regimental chaplain who led the service, said poignantly, 'We feel every death in our regiment. Just because it's not the same cap badge it doesn't make it any less painful.' Hundreds of well-wishers clapped and cheered as the troops filed past. Was this what it was like for their brothers in arms of generations past? Certainly Harry, who had already compared his frontline service to that experienced by World War II soldiers, thought so. As he marched, some people hung out of windows of their houses to catch a glimpse of the troops and the prince in their throng.

Harry had been quick to dismiss talk of his personal heroics. Of course he was right to point out that real heroes of any conflict are those injured in the line of duty or those who never return home to their loved ones; the ones who make the ultimate sacrifice for their country. But their suffering and the pain of their families should not detract from Harry's achievement. A hero is, after all, someone who is distinguished for his or her courage or ability; someone who is admired for brave deeds and noble qualities. They may have performed heroic acts. They may also be someone who is a model or an ideal; and Harry certainly lived up to that too. Just because the prince was not injured in the line of fire and forced to return home early does not mean his achievement was any less.

The prince had certainly proved himself and showed the true courage of a soldier. He had willingly put his royal neck on the line and demonstrated to everyone – including his army of detractors, who somehow believed he had never been in danger despite the evidence to the contrary – what he was made of. He had proved he had the courage of his convictions, both to himself and to them. The Prince could have taken the easy option but it was not in his nature. He had gone to war because it was his duty to do so. He had gone to war because it was his job to stand shoulder to shoulder with his men. He went to the frontline knowing his royal status made him a trophy target; knowing that Al Qaeda and Taliban commanders had vowed to kidnap him, slice off his ears, kill him and return his dead body to the Queen. Harry had been honest enough to admit he was scared, yet he had faced his fears and showed the men he served alongside that he had the mettle and strength to stand with them when it mattered. He was proud to serve with them and them with him.

Corporal Andrew Marsh, 37, who had served alongside Harry, collected his medal too on 5 May. He said: 'To see everybody cheering and waving for you is incredible.' Staff Corporal Alan Hughes, 39, added: 'Harry is an outstanding soldier and did Britain proud. He's a top bloke.' Corporal David Baxter – Prince Harry's partner in the air control team – was among those at the ceremony and service. The 28-year-old from Coleraine, Northern Ireland, praised Harry too, saying he was disappointed that the prince's deployment had been cut short. 'It doubled up the workload that we had and every time we had a major operation we had to get someone to replace him. A lot of people were disappointed about it that he did have to go.' He added: 'He was just one of the lads.' Their comments must have been music to Harry's ears. He could not have wished for a greater commendation.

Harry wanted to do more. Two days after his medal

presentation he and William led London in honouring our wounded heroes. They cheered our battle scarred servicemen, including the man he had called one of the 'real heroes' of the Afghan conflict, Royal Marine Ben McBean, at the City Salute outside St Paul's Cathedral. Harry may have delighted in being 'just one of the lads' but like his mother – who had similarly craved normality – he knew his status meant he had the chance to do more to help those who needed his help. The royal brothers pledged to do all they could after seeing first hand the plight of neglected servicemen. And in just three months as patrons of the appeal they helped to secure £850,000 to help our heroes.

In a joint statement the princes praised the 'remarkable qualities' of our servicemen and women. 'Their professionalism is coupled with quite extraordinary personal qualities of courage, resilience, modesty and humour – qualities which they display in good times and in bad, and which are humbling and inspiring beyond measure.' They were talking about men like Corporal Bryan Budd of 3 Para, killed in action in Helmand and posthumously awarded the Victoria Cross. He died on 20 August 2006, fifteen months before Harry arrived in Helmand, leading from the front and making the ultimate sacrifice to save his men. He charged into oncoming fire after spotting a group of Taliban fighters. Budd made a split-second decision that cost him his life, but it saved those of his men. He charged forward through the vegetation, firing as he went. It gave his men just enough time to crawl away to safety. His story of self-sacrifice was remarkable, but exemplified the true courage of our soldiers.

When Harry dismissed talk of his heroics, he was

thinking of men like Bryan Budd. But the prince's courage should not be dismissed. His frontline service was the nearest, in modern conditions, that a prince could get to the scene in Shakespeare's Henry V when the King moves among his men in disguise on the eve of battle, sharing, talking, listening – 'a little touch of Harry in the night'. Some have argued that the fight in Afghanistan was a very controversial war, and therefore one that was too dangerous for the British Royal Family to be associated with. But the Army he served in is not fighting some mythical crusade in Afghanistan; it was simply targeting terrorists who threatened peace and freedom.

His service undoubtedly strengthened the monarchy's links with the people of this country and raised his personal standing among those who had dismissed him as a playboy prince of little substance. Until he had been sent on combat operations, many would have suggested that there was one rule for members of the Royal Family and another for the rest of the Armed Forces. Some claimed his training had been a complete waste of money. That was certainly the impression given by the Government and the Army when it was ruled that deploying Harry to Iraq was too great a risk both to him and his fellow soldiers. But the prince would not let it rest and it is to his credit.

He would not have been the first returning officer whose thoughts had drifted to the words of the eighteenth-century essayist Dr Samuel Johnson, who famously wrote that 'Every man thinks meanly of himself for not having been a soldier.' It is also true that every soldier thinks just as meanly of himself if he has not heard the sound of gun fire in theatre. Harry's great-grandmother, the Queen Mother, famously welcomed the German bomb that fell on Buckingham Palace during the Blitz in 1940. She declared she could now 'look the East End in the eye'. Through his own gritty, some would say bloody-minded, determination Harry was now able to look every soldier in the eye. Indeed, the soldier-prince can look the whole country in the eye.

GLOSSARY

al-Qaeda: international terrorist network founded by
               Osama Bin Laden (Arabic for 'the base' or
               'the camp')
ANP: Afghan National Police
Bergen: type of backpack used by soldiers
BFBS: British Forces Broadcasting Service
FAC: forward air controller
FOB: forward operating base
HESCO: blast-proof wire-mesh cage filled with
               rubble and topped with corrugated iron,
               named after HESCO Bastion, the British
               company that produces it; used for
               fortification
IED: improvised explosive device (usually a mine
               intended to blow up vehicles)
JTAC: Joint Tactical Air Coordination (JTAC Hill
               is a former British Empire fort built in
               1841); also joint terminal attack controller

Kevlar: reinforced material used in, e.g., bulletproof vests

kukri: large knife whose blade broadens towards its point, used by Ghurkhas

madrasa: an Islamic school

ROZ: restricted operation zone

RPG: rocket-propelled grenade

SAS: Special Air Services, an elite, specialist regiment of the British Army trained in commando techniques and clandestine operations

Taliban: Islamist fundamentalist organisation created in 1994 that was the unofficial government of most of Afghanistan from 1996 to 2001